LGBTQ Youth Issues

A practical guide for youth workers
serving lesbian, gay, bisexual,
transgender, and questioning youth

Gerald P. Mallon DSW

CWLA
PRESS

CWLA Headquarters
1726 M St. NW, Suite 500
Washington, DC 20036
www.cwla.org

CURRENT PRINTING (last digit)
10 9 8 7 6 5 4 3 2

Cover and text design by Tim Murren
Cover photograph by Meredith Rishel
Edited by Meghan Williams

Printed in the United States of America

ISBN: 978-158760-138-5

Library of Congress Cataloging-in-Publication Data
Mallon, Gerald P.
  LGBTQ youth issues : a practical guide for youth workers serving lesbian, gay, bisexual, transgender, and questioning youth / Gerald P. Mallon.
       p. cm.
  Earlier ed. under title: Lesbian and gay youth issues.
  Includes bibliographical references.
  ISBN 978-1-58760-138-5 (alk. paper)
 1. Social work with gay youth. 2. Social work with transgender youth.
3. Social work with bisexuals. 4. Gay youth--Psychology. 5. Transgender
youth--Psychology. 6. Bisexual youth--Psychology. I. Mallon, Gerald P.
Lesbian and gay youth issues. II. Title.
  HV1426.M347 2010
  362.7--dc22

                                                        2010031217

For Binho, meu amor, minha vida, meu mundo

Table of Contents

Acknowledgements

U sually after a book is published, I never look at it again.
What was done long ago or yesterday is old business, and
my hope is for the future—what is ahead, and not what happened in the past. Looking back either makes me see too many
errors, or makes me feel too good about what I have done. But
in revising this book, which was originally written almost 10
years ago, I was reminded that I said then that this book was a
labor of love and a pleasure to write. I still feel the same way—
no need to say it all again.

There are of course several people whom I would like to
thank for helping to make this possible. Foremost, I am grateful to the many fine colleagues that I have had the privilege of
working with over the years at CWLA. CWLA has always been
supportive of the work that I have done with LGBTQ youth and
their families, and for their collaboration I am deeply grateful.

I am grateful too to my many wonderful colleagues at one of
the finest schools of social work in the country—The Hunter
College School of Social Work—and my wonderful colleagues
at the National Resource Center for Permanency and Family
Connections and the Children's Bureau Training and Technical
Assistance Network, for allowing me to be part of several nurturing environments and for giving me more than one place to
call home.

To my friends and my family who love me and give me a life
and meaning outside of my work, my thanks is inestimable.

Introduction: Preparing to Work with LGBTQ Youth

> I'm sure we must have some gay or lesbian youth in
> our program, but come to think of it, I don't think that
> I have ever had any that have come out to me.
> —Training participant at a child welfare agency

This book is designed to help youth care providers increase
their knowledge about and skills in working with lesbian,
gay, bisexual, transgender, and questioning (LGBTQ) youth and
their families. LGBTQ children and youth, and families affected by issues of gender or sexual orientation, are present in
every youth service agency in this country, but because most
professionals do not have adequate knowledge about an
LGBTQ orientation, this is often an invisible population. Consequently, most youth workers (including supervisors, managers, and administrators), unless they are LGBTQ themselves
or have a highly developed knowledge base about working with
these clients, are not usually well prepared to address or respond to these clients' needs.

Although LGBTQ youth remain invisible populations for
many, the reality is, if you work with adolescents, then you are

already working with LGBTQ youth. This book, which consists of
12 chapters and a detailed resources list, is designed to provide
workers with accurate basic information about and actual case
examples of LGBTQ youth and their families. All chapters also
include a section called "What Can Youth Workers Do?" (in
some chapters, it is "What Can Youth-Serving Agencies Do?")
that shares strategies and concrete actions youth workers can
take to help LGBTQ youth.

In an easy-to-read, question-and-answer format, the first
chapter provides readers with information about the basics of
working with LGBTQ youth. Chapter 2 focuses on the critical
issues surrounding the coming out process for LGBT youth.
Family issues, including foster/adoptive family issues, are the
central focus in Chapter 3. Chapter 4 examines discrimination
and anti-LGBTQ violence. The need to create healthy social
environments for LGBTQ youth is explored in Chapter 5. In
Chapter 6, I review the central developmental appropriateness
of relationships and dating. Chapters 7, 8, and 9 specifically
look at an array of unique issues for LGBTQ youth and youth
workers in schools, health and mental health settings, and out-
of-home care, respectively. Chapters 10 and 11 examine special populations of youth in the LGBTQ community; Chapter
10 focuses on transgender youth, while Chapter 11 looks at
homeless youth, questioning youth, and LBGTQ youth of color.
The final chapter examines what steps organizations can take
to change their cultures and become LGBTQ-affirming agencies. Books and other publications directly referred to in the
text are cited in the References section. A resources list of
websites and programs are found at the conclusion of the book;
bear in mind that the availability of resources like these
changes rapidly.

This guide is written from an LGBTQ-affirming perspective
of sexual and gender orientation, which views LGBTQ identity
from an amoral position—as a natural and normal variation of
sexual or gender orientation, which is not pathologized. The data presented herein is practice-based evidence, representative
of the current thinking of leading experts practicing with, and in

many cases researching, LGBTQ youth and their families. The case examples utilized to illustrate points throughout represent actual LGBTQ youth with whom I have had the opportunity to work. These cases, which exemplify the actual experiences of youth in a wide variety of youth service settings, were gathered as part of my work as a consultant, trainer, researcher, and practitioner around the United States and in Canada. The names of these young people and were altered to protect their confidentiality, and agency names have been removed.

Explanation of Terms

As with any youth-oriented culture, lesbian, gay, bisexual, transgender, and questioning (LGBTQ) youth have their own unique language, and an ability to speak their language is essential. The language of LGBTQ youth makes many adults uncomfortable, but to be effective in working with them, adults must overcome their discomfort and become familiar with the terms that LGBTQ youth use to define themselves. Workers may also want to utilize online slang dictionaries, which cover both complimentary and offensive terms, to keep up with the changing lexicon. Listed below are several key terms that will assist youth workers in this process at this point in time.

This glossary is intended to orient the reader to the more commonly used vocabulary in LGBTQ literature, culture, and speech. Language is often a source of confusion and misinformation and as such, it is important that service providers have accurate definitions. Heterosexually oriented care providers are often unfamiliar and uncomfortable with the vernacular of the LGBTQ culture. It should be recognized that, as with any subculture—particularly oppressed groups—there is a constantly changing argot. Usage may vary with generation, area of the country, socioeconomic status, or cultural background.

It should also be noted that LGBTQ youth first coming to terms with their emerging gender or sexual orientation may not use these terms to define themselves—they might say, "I like boys, like that—you know?" The following terms should also never be used for youth just coming to terms with their identities in a direct, confrontational manner, like "Are you gay?" or "Are you bisexual?" But with this in mind, professionals need to know what the appropriate terms in the 21st Century are and be able to comfortably use them in working with youth and their families.

The language in this publication is intended to be understandable and acceptable. *Same-sex, gay, lesbian, heterosexual, transgender*, and *bisexual* are used to describe sexuality and partnerships. While no one owns definitions, many of the definitions below are based on previous work developed by Mallon & Betts (2005). For images of the described symbols, see the inside back cover of this book.

General Terms

Sex, Gender, and Sexuality

The English noun *gender* is derived from the Old French word *genre*, meaning "kind of thing." It goes back to the Latin word *genus* (meaning "kind" or "species"). *Gender* is often, but decreasingly, used as a synonym for *sex*, which refers to the physical anatomical differences that are commonly used to differentiate male from female.

Many people, among them social scientists, use *sex* to refer to the biological division into male and female, and *gender* to refer to social roles assigned to people on the basis of their apparent sex and other associated factors. Society tends to assign some social roles to males and others to females, based on how society perceives their sex.

A birth certificate describes a newborn's sex, which is sometimes viewed as assigning gender. The terms *male* or *female* recorded on the birth certificate can affect much of what happens to that child, socially, for the rest of his or her life.

Gender is social, cultural, psychological, and historical. It is used to describe people and their roles in society, the way they dress, and how they are meant to behave (see Colapinto, 2000, for a riveting discussion about gender).

It is assumed by some that sex, gender, and sexuality naturally follow on from each other, but different societies and cultures have had very different notions of sex, gender, and sexuality, and how people express them. It is perhaps more helpful to consider "What is sexuality, and how do people in different places and at different times understand their bodies and desires?" *Sexuality* is usually defined as the expression of sexual desire.

Sexual Orientation

This is the commonly accepted term for the direction of a person's sexual attraction, emotional or physical attraction, and its expression. Examples of sexual orientation are heterosexuality, homosexuality, and bisexuality. In a sense, sexual orientation is a social construct, and a relatively new one, most likely determined by a combination of continually interacting sociocultural influences and biological tendencies.

For many years, the common assumption—shared by many scientists and religious communities—was that the natural and normal human sexual orientation is exclusively for the opposite sex (i.e., heterosexual). The historian Michel Foucault (1976) argued that homosexuality as a concept did not exist as such in the 18th Century, when people instead spoke of sodomy, which involved specific sexual acts, regardless of the sex or sexuality of the people involved. Sexual studies carried out during and after the 1950s (Hooker, 1957, 1967) led psychologists and doctors to recognize homosexuality as a second exclusive orientation. Since then, similar acceptance has grown for nonexclusive orientations, such as bisexuality.

Heterosexuality

This term relates to sexual attraction, both physical and emotional, which is primarily directed toward people of the opposite gender.

Homosexuality

This term relates to sexual attraction, both physical and emotional, which is primarily directed toward people of the same gender. The word *homosexual* translates literally as "of the same sex," being a hybrid of the Greek prefix *homo-* meaning "same" (as distinguished from the Latin root *homo* meaning "human") and the Latin root *sex* meaning "sex."

Although some early writers used the adjective *homosexual* to refer to any single-gender context (such as an all-girls school), today the term implies a sexual aspect. The term *homosocial* is now used to describe single-sex contexts that are not specifically sexual. Older terms for homosexuality, such as *homophilia* and *inversion* (in which a gay individual would be called a "homophile" or an "invert") have fallen into disuse. The term *homosexual* can be used as a noun or adjective to describe same-sex-oriented individuals as well as their sexual attractions and behaviors.

It is recommend that the terms *homosexual* and *homosexuality* be avoided. In particular, describing individuals as homosexual may be offensive, due to the term's history. There is a negative clinical association of the word, stemming from its use in describing same-sex attraction as a pathological state when homosexuality was included in lists of mental disorders. It was not until the late 1980s that journals began to focus on research and articles that were LGBT-affirming in their approach to treatment and practice with LGBT people.

Bisexuality

This term refers to sexual attraction toward people of both genders. Someone who identifies as bisexual is attracted to and may form sexual and affectionate relationships with both men and women, though not necessarily at the same time. The term may refer to a sociopolitical identity or to sexual behavior, or both. Most known societies have included people who have exhibited some degree of bisexuality.

Although bisexuality is an identified sexual orientation, it is sometimes transitional for those coming to terms with their lesbian or gay identity. Some people identify as bisexual before identifying as gay or lesbian, because bisexuality can represent a transitional, mediating position between homosexual and heterosexual in the traditional cultural system.

Homosexual

The use of the word *homosexual* in describing individuals and same-sex relationships may be inaccurate. When referring to people, as opposed to behavior, *homosexual* is considered derogatory and places the emphasis on sex. The preferred terms used by most are *gay* and *lesbian*, which stress cultural and social matters more than sex. In addition, prior to 1972, the term *homosexual* was a diagnostic term used to pathologize gay men and lesbians.

Gay

In addition to meaning "merry," "joyous," or "glad," *gay* also means homosexual. *Gay* also refers to ideas (e.g., literature or values). The word *gay* has had a sexual meaning since at least the 19th Century (and possibly earlier; Chauncey, 1995). In Victorian England, female and male prostitutes were called "gay" because they dressed gaily—wearing bright, noticeable clothing. Eventually, *gay boys* (male prostitutes) became used as a term for any male homosexual. It has also been claimed that *gay* was an acronym for "Good As You"; another popular etymology has the word's supposed origin being from Gay Street, in New York's West Village, a focal point of lesbian and gay culture. The term also seems, from documentary evidence, to have existed in New York as a code word in the 1940s, where the question, "Are you gay?" would denote more than it might have seemed to outsiders (Chauncey, 1995).

Gay can be used to refer only to males who are other than heterosexually oriented, but is often used inclusively to refer to men and women who identify as such, and arguably to bisexuals as well. When used in the phrase *the gay community*, it may also be used a broad and inclusive term meant to include lesbians, bisexuals, and questioning and transgender people.

However, in this text, the terms *lesbian, gay, bisexual, transgender*, and *questioning* (LGBTQ) are intentionally used.

Gay originally was used purely as an adjective ("He is a gay man" or "He is gay"). *Gay* is now also used as a collective noun (e.g., "Gays are opposed to that policy"), but rarely as a singular noun ("He is a gay"). When used as an adjective not describing a person who is part of the gay community—as many children and youth are now popularizing in school settings; e.g., "That shirt is so gay"—the term *gay* is purely pejorative and deeply offensive. The derogatory implication is that the object (or person) in question is inferior, weak, effeminate, or less than.

Lesbian

A lesbian is a woman whose sexual orientation is self-defined, affirmed, or acknowledged as such. *Lesbian* also refers to a female who is other than heterosexually oriented (and can refer to women-oriented) ideas, communities, or varieties of cultural expression.

The word *lesbian* originally referred to an inhabitant of the Greek island of Lesbos. It came to have its current meaning because of the ancient Greek poet Sappho, who lived on Lesbos; some of her poems concerned love between women. Whether Sappho was a lesbian, in the modern meaning of the term, or simply a poet who described lesbians is open to question. Nevertheless, this association with Sappho led to the term *sapphism* being used as another term for lesbianism.

Transgender

Transgender is now generally considered an umbrella term encompassing many different identities. It is commonly used to describe an individual who is seen as "gender-different."

Transgender is often used as a euphemistic synonym for transsexual people—although this term *transsexual* has fallen out of favor as a useful term by many transgender people. *Transgender* is also used to describe behavior or feelings that cannot be categorized into other defined categories; for example, people living in a gender role that is different from the one they were assigned at birth, but who do not wish to undergo any or all of the available medical options, or people who do not wish to identify themselves as transsexuals, either men or women, and consider that they fall between genders or transcend gender. By using the words *transgender* and/or *trans* in this text, I seek to establish a common language, and I am not seeking to erase any of the diverse identities of individuals in this subculture.

To further expand their knowledge in working with this population, readers should see Brill & Pepper (2008); Currah, Juang, & Minter (2006); Davis (2008); DeCrescenzo & Mallon (2000); Glenn (2009); Israel & Tarver (1998); Lev (2004); Mallon (2009); Mallon & DeCrescenzo (2008); and Pazos (2009).

Questioning

This is a term used to identify a cluster of young people who are unsure of their sexual orientation. In my own clinical practice, I have seen three types of questioning youth, although I am sure that there are youth workers who may have worked with other youth who are questioning. These are:

- Youth who are "going through a phase" or experimenting. This may be due to a specific living situation, such as a same-gendered group home, juvenile justice facility, or even high school. The term *situational homosexuality* is explained in Chapter 1.
- Youth who have experienced but may have not disclosed sexual abuse perpetrated by adults, particularly by adults of their same sex.
- Youth who may have a serious psychiatric condition, and claim an LGBT identity to "fit in."

Heterosexism (or Heterocentrism, or Heterosexualism)

These terms, all of which are interchangeable, describe the assumption that everyone or a particular person is heterosexual. It does not necessarily imply hostility toward other sexual orientations (as does *homophobia*), but is merely a failure to recognize

their existence. Heterocentrism is culturally, religiously, and socially sanctioned by most major institutions in American culture, including the family.

Homophobia

This term is most frequently used to describe any sort of opposition to homosexual behavior or the political causes associated
with homosexuality, though this opposition may more accurately
be called "anti-gay bias."

The term also describes a phobia triggered by an encounter
(in oneself or others) with same-sex physical attraction, love,
and sexuality. The term was originally described by George
Weinberg (1972), the clinical psychologist who coined the
term, to mean a morbid and irrational fear of homosexuals.

Homo-ignorant

Homo-ignorant is a term developed to describe individuals
with a very limited knowledge about LGBTQ individuals.

Transvestite/Cross-Dresser

This is a person who, for any reason, wears the clothing of a
gender other than that to which they were assigned at birth.
Cross-dressers may have no desire or intention of adopting the
behaviors or practices common to that other gender and do not
necessarily wish to undergo medical procedures to facilitate
physical changes. Contrary to common belief, most male-bodied
cross-dressers prefer female partners.

Drag

The term *drag queen* originates in Polari, the language of gay
men in England in the early part of the 20th Century. *Drag*
meant "clothes," and was also theatre slang for a woman's cos-
tume worn by a male actor. A *queen* is an effeminate gay man.

Drag is a part of Western gay culture—drag involves wearing highly exaggerated and outrageous costumes or imitating
movie and music stars of the opposite sex. It is a form of per-
forming art practiced by drag queens and kings. Female-bodied

people who perform in usually exaggerated men's clothes and personae are called *drag kings*, though this term has a wider meaning than *drag queens*. Drag kings should not just be seen as female equivalents of drag queens, because the term covers a much wider field of gender performance and political activism. Gender identity among drag kings is far more varied, too. Drag kings are largely a phenomenon of lesbian culture; they have only recently begun to gain the fame or focus that drag queens have known for years.

LGBTQ-Affirming Practice

LGBTQ-affirmative practice is a culturally sensitive model for working with LGBTQ people. This model views LGBTQ identity through an affirming and nonpathological lens. It is a description of practices that arises out of the context of a dominant culture in society, which attempts to regulate and specify according to normative notions of gender and sexuality. It arises out of a discourse of power that asks questions about how operations of power have been and are carried out. LGBTQ-affirming practice encourages an idea of a constantly evolving relationship between theory and practice. It recognizes the influences on our thinking and practice of different contexts such as race, culture, class, ability, gender, and sexuality.

Culture-Specific Terms and Symbols

Coming Out

Coming out is defined as "the developmental process through which LGBT people recognize their gender or sexual orientation and integrate this knowledge into their personal and social lives" (De Monteflores & Schultz, 1978, p. 59). A distinctively LGBT phenomenon (see Cass, 1979, 1984; Coleman, 1981; Troiden, 1979, 1993), it is the process of first recognizing and then acknowledging nonheterosexual orientation in oneself, and then disclosing it to others. Coming out often occurs in stages and is a nonlinear process. Because coming out is a process, the individual needs to proceed at his or her pace. An individual may decide to come out to certain people and not others. Some may never come out to anyone beside themselves. *Coming out* can also be used to mean *disclosure*, as in "I just came out to my parents."

Disclosure

The point at which an LGBT person discloses his or her gender or sexual orientation, first to him- or herself, and then to another person. It is not appropriate to use terms such as *discovered, admitted, revealed, found out,* or *declared,* which are pejorative terms, suggesting judgment.

Out

This term is used to describe a person who openly acknowledges his or her gender/sexual orientation to friends, family, colleagues, and society. Not everyone who is *out* is out to all of these groups. Some people may be out to their friends, but not to their family. Others are out privately, but not to colleagues at work.

Closeted or In the Closet

These terms refer to someone who is not open about his or her sexual orientation. This person, for his or her own personal reasons, chooses to hide his or her orientation from others.

Stonewall

The Stonewall Rebellion of 1969 is widely considered the beginning of the modern LGBT rights movement. The six-day riot, which began inside of the Stonewall Inn in the Greenwich Village neighborhood of New York City, was the breaking point of years of tensions between police and lesbian, gay, bisexual, and transgender street youth.

The 1960's were a heightened time for human and civil rights issues for many marginalized populations in the United States. LGBT people grew increasingly intolerant of continued harassment and arrests by police. At the time, LGBT people were subjected to civil laws that criminalized sodomy and, in New York City, allowed bars to refuse service to LGBT patrons. Arrests, harassment, and instances of entrapment by police were frequent. Civil laws reinforced their actions. In establishments where LGBT patrons were served, they were often entrapped by plainclothes police officers, posing as regular bar patrons. Transgender people were openly arrested on the streets.

One establishment where LGBT patrons found refuge was the Stonewall Inn. To enter, bar goers paid a $3 cover and signed a register (often with a fictitious or humorous name). The management was often tipped off when the local police district planned a raid on the bar and would warn LGBT patrons by turning on the lights or operating a buzzer and blinking light in the ceiling of the bar.

On the morning of June 28, 1969, without the usual tip off, the New York City Police Department raided the bar. The drag queens and street youth fought back. There were reports of shoes, bottles, coins, bricks, and debris thrown. The altercation spilled into the streets and more LGBT street youth joined in the uprising. As word spread, more LGBT people from surrounding neighborhoods joined the riot. The rebellion, which lasted six days, marked the beginning of the modern LGBT rights movement.

Reclaimed Negative Terms

Words including *queer*, *dyke*, and *faggot* are sometimes used to refer negatively to LGBTQ people. They are equivalent to hate terms and epithets used against racial and ethnic minorities.

A political usage exists for words like these by some LGBT people who, in a reclamation process, redefine and use with pride words formerly used in a pejorative way. Because these words still carry a negative connotation in society, however, their positive usage is restricted to political LGBT people active in the reclamation struggle and as words used by in-group members to define themselves.

Lambda

The eleventh letter of the Greek alphabet. The lambda was first chosen as a gay symbol when it was adopted in 1970 by the New York Gay Activists Alliance. It became the symbol of their growing movement of gay liberation. In 1974, the lambda was subsequently adopted by the International Gay Rights Congress held in Edinburgh, Scotland. As their symbol for lesbian and gay rights, the lambda has become internationally popular.

Pink triangle

In Nazi Germany, homosexuals were forced to wear the pink triangle and were treated as the lowest status individuals by the Nazis. Gay men have reclaimed the pink triangle and wear it as a badge of honor and also as a symbol of militancy against institutionalized oppression.

Black triangle

The black triangle was used to identify those the Nazis deemed "socially unacceptable" women. Lesbians were included in this classification. Now, lesbians have reclaimed the black triangle as a symbol in defiance of repression and discrimination, just as gay men have reclaimed the pink triangle.

Intertwined male genetic symbol

This variation of a traditional symbol identifies gay men.

Intertwined female genetic symbol

This variation of a traditional symbol identifies lesbians.

Labrys

The labrys is less popular now than it once was, even though its connection to lesbianism and women began thousands of years ago. The labrys is basically a double bladed axe or hatchet that can be used for both harvesting and as a weapon. It was favored by tribes of female Amazons that roamed the area around what is now Kazakstan in central Asia. Today, the labrys has become a symbol of lesbian and feminist strength and self-sufficiency.

Transgender symbol

The International Foundation for Gender Education logo, or transgender symbol, is the widely recognized symbol for cross-dressers, transvestites, transsexuals, and transgenderists. The logo is purple overlapping genetic symbols imposed on a pink triangle.

Rainbow flag

Created in 1978 for San Francisco's Gay Freedom Celebration by Gilbert Baker, the flag depicts not the shape of the rainbow, but its colors in horizontal stripes. The rainbow flag has been adopted as the LGBT flag, and traditionally includes six colors—leaving out violet—with red at the top. It represents the diversity yet unity of LGBT people universally.

Freedom rings

Designed by David Spada with the rainbow flag in mind, these are six colored aluminum rings. They have come to symbolize independence and tolerance of others. Freedom rings are frequently worn as necklaces, bracelets, rings, and key chains. Recently, freedom triangles have emerged as a popular alternative to the rings, though the meaning remains the same.

1

The Basics

Can Youth Really Be LGBT?

> If you are a teenager and you say that you're gay, you
> are told that you are not gay and that you're going
> through a phase because you are a teenager. Or you're
> told that you are mixed up and that once you come out
> of this stage, (you know as a teenager you are sup-
> posed to go through these stages) then you will not be
> gay. That's their attitude! If we know, that we know,
> that we know, that we know, that we know, that we
> know, that we are gay, they still tell us that we're not,
> it's just a phase. I think that they don't want to believe
> that young people can be gay.

The quote above, taken from my book *We Don't Exactly Get the Welcome Wagon* (Mallon, 1998b), aptly expresses one young man's frustration in getting adults to believe that he is gay. Youth workers can probably relate to this situation, as sure-ly many have asked themselves at one time or another: Is this youth really gay, or is he or she just going through a phase?

Although many adolescents verbalize confusion about their sexual identity or experiment—which is usually expressed through sexual behavior—it is important to remember that sexual behavior alone does not constitute a lesbian, gay, bisexual, transgender, or questioning (LGBTQ) identity. While some teens will experiment with same-gender sexual behavior (see the definition for *questioning*) others are very clear about their orientation as gay, lesbian, bisexual, or transgender individuals.

As society is gradually becoming more affirming about the experiences of LGBTQ people (as evidenced by LGBTQ characters on TV, in books, and in films), LGBTQ youth are afforded greater opportunities to see visible images of their lives. As a consequence, some LGBTQ youth are beginning to feel more comfortable coming out at earlier ages.

In my own practice, I have worked with youth that are clear about their identity as an LGBT individual as young as age 10. Therefore—yes, it is very possible for an LGBT youth to be sure about who they are.

It is also possible for some youth to not be certain about their gender or sexual orientation and those youth may go back and forth between self-identifying as lesbian or gay, bisexual, transgender, straight, and back again. Dealing with gender or sexual identity ambiguity makes many adults uncomfortable, but gaining a greater comfort with this ambiguity is necessary for youth workers.

In preparing the revision of this book I wanted to deal with some of the questions that I know youth workers must have about LGBTQ youth. In the absence of accurate information, many professionals rely on their own knowledge, which is often based on stereotypes and myths about LGBTQ people. What follows is a series of questions and answers about LGBTQ people that will replace some of those erroneous assumptions with valid, accurate, and relevant information about LGBTQ youth.

How do you know if you're lesbian, gay, bisexual, or transgender?

For the most part, knowing whether you're LGBT is all about paying attention to feelings of attraction. It is very difficult for

many people to be honest with themselves about same-gender attraction because society is, in general, so unaccepting of them.

Some youth know that they are LGBT early in life—as early
as 10 years old. Others do not acknowledge these feelings until
much later. Coming out, as we shall see in the next chapter,
can occur at any time in the life cycle, not just during childhood or adolescence.

Can someone be LGBT without ever having had an LGBT experience or relationship?

Yes. In fact, many of the LGBTQ youth with whom you have
worked or will work have never engaged in a sexual relationship with another person and yet they know that they are gay,
lesbian, bisexual, or transgender. Sexual orientation has more
to do with internal feelings—one's sense of "fit"—rather than
actual sexual experience.

Can someone have LGBT feelings and not be LGBT? Can someone have heterosexual feelings and not be a heterosexual?

Yes. Human sexuality is very complex and not easily separat-
ed into rigid categories. It is perfectly normal for a lesbian or
gay person to have feelings of attraction for someone of the
opposite gender, just as it is perfectly normal for a heterosexual person to have feelings for a person of the same gender.
Although almost everyone experiences these feelings at one
time or another, usually during adolescence, they can still be
confusing. Many youth struggling with issues of sexual orientation will test out their feelings with both males and females.
In some colleges there is a term known as *lesbian until gradu-
ation*, or LUG, used to describe the same-gender relationships
that some women are involved in. Again, it is important to remember that youth will eventually "be who they are." Nothing
that anyone tells them or says to encourage them or dissuade
them will change their actual sexual or gender orientation.

Sexuality and sexual/gender identity is a very complex and complicated arena of practice. Therefore, all youth workers must develop skills for dealing with the ambiguity of gender and sexual identity. This may require that you look deep into yourself as a worker and a person, to determine your own feelings, thoughts, and experiences with respect to gender and sexual orientation.

If you have had a same-gender sexual experience, does that make you LGBT?

No—being LGBT is not just about sexual behavior. The sexual aspect of an LGBT youth's life is of course important, but to focus exclusively on those aspects is a mistake. In fact, as described above, many LGBTQ youth who are dealing with issues of sexual/gender orientation have never engaged in sexual behavior at all, either with opposite- or same-gender partners.

Knowing that you are gay, lesbian, bisexual, or transgender is more than just sexual behavior. It is about your sense of internal goodness of fit. One young man quoted here and also in other places in this book described it this way:

> When I was trying to figure things out about whether I was gay, I first dated girls, then boys, then girls, and somewhere along the line it just felt better with boys. I don't mean the sex, because I was then and still am a virgin, but it's kinda like trying on a pair of gloves. You know, if you put the left glove on the right hand it fits, but somehow it doesn't feel right. Then when you switch it to the right hand where it belongs, you know that you have a good fit—because it feels right. No one has to tell you that it feels right, because really no one really knows except for you. That's what makes it hard, you really have to do a lot of figuring it out, all by yourself.

In working with LGBTQ youth, youth workers need to be clear—both for themselves and their young clients—that

gender/sexual orientation and sexuality involve many aspects
of identity and relationship that go beyond sexual behavior.

Many heterosexual people have engaged in same-gender
sexual behavior and vice-versa. These experiences do not
change anyone's core gender/sexual orientation.

What is "situational homosexuality"?

In certain same-gender only environments (i.e., group homes,
large congregate care child welfare placements, all-boy or all-
girl boarding schools, prisons, some religious communities, and
the military) individuals will engage in same-gender sexual behavior. For these individuals, their sexual orientation remains
the same; they are heterosexual and given the opportunity they
would choose an opposite-gender partner. These individuals
are sometimes erroneously labeled as bisexuals, but they are
generally not bisexuals. Some may be questioning, but most are
probably heterosexually identified youth who engage in same-
sex sexuality due to the nature of their circumstances.

How many LGBTQ people are there?

Although there has been a great deal of discussion about the
quantification of LGBTQ people, the reality is that since it is
still stigmatizing for people to identify as such, most LGBTQ
people are socialized to hide (Martin & Hetrick, 1998). Since
most LGBTQ people—especially youth—continue to hide,
mostly for safety reasons, it is very difficult to ascertain how
many LGBTQ people there are. The commonly accepted figure
is that 1 in 10 people are LGBTQ. This is based on Alfred Kinsey's studies from 1948 and 1953 (Kinsey, Pomeroy, & Martin,
1948; Kinsey, Pomeroy, Martin, & Gebhardt, 1953). There has
been no definitive study conducted since then to confirm or re-
fute these findings. Nonetheless, regardless of how many
LGBTQ people there are, it is safe to say that every youth service agency in the United States has worked with some youth
that identify as such.

Have there always been LGBTQ people?

Yes. There is evidence of the existence of LGBT people throughout history, as depicted in art, literature, and music.

How do you become LGBTQ?

You cannot *become* an LGBTQ person, any more than a person *becomes* heterosexual. Since sexual identity emanates from an internal sense of fit, most LGBTQ people become aware of these feelings as they grow. Exactly where these feelings come from and why remains an unknown factor.

Are some people born gay, lesbian, bisexual, or transgender?

According to some researchers, there is preliminary empirical evidence that strongly suggests a genetic and biological basis for male sexual orientation and a few studies suggest the same for female sexual orientation. Although many gay males, some bisexuals, some transgender people, and some lesbians recall that they have always known that they were "different," others do not agree with the "gay from birth" philosophy. Again, the research in this area is very limited. Youth workers interested in this topic should review research on this topic, including Hamer, Hu, Magnuson, Hu, & Pattatucci (1993); LeVay (1993); LeVay, Baldwin, & Baldwin (2009); and McFadden & Pasanen (1998).

Is being gay, lesbian, bisexual, or transgender a choice for some people?

Just as heterosexual people do not choose their sexual orientation, the large majority of LGBT people do not choose theirs. The only real choice that most LGBT people have to deal with is whether to be open about their orientation with others. Some LGBT people, however, do envision their entire identity as a social construction—a series of choices that one makes about constructing his or her life.

Can someone be seduced into being LGBT?

No, it is simply not possible for someone to be seduced into being LGBT any more than an LGBT person could be seduced into being heterosexual.

Do LGBTQ people recruit others to become like them?

No. I think what does happen sometimes in youth work is that a youth who may be struggling with issues of an LGBT identity meets another LGBT youth who is open about his or her identity, and the first youth realizes that he or she might be able to be open and out too. There is strength in numbers, so having a peer who is also LGBT can be a wonderful support system for someone who is internally struggling with the same issues. This occurrence might make someone believe that the "formerly heterosexual" youth was recruited, but this is simply not possible.

Are LGBT people more likely to be more promiscuous than heterosexual people?

LGBT people are neither more or less sexually promiscuous than heterosexuals. Like heterosexuals, many LGBT people are involved in monogamous relationships, considering themselves partners and committed to each other for life. Some LGBT people may also choose to remain celibate, and others may have multiple partners, just as some heterosexuals do. There is no scientific evidence to suggest that LGBT people are any more promiscuous than are heterosexually oriented people.

Are LGBT people more likely to molest a child?

No. Offenders are more likely to be male relatives or acquaintances of their victim than strangers. But despite clear evidence, there are many people who continue to promote the misconception that being LGBT means someone is more likely to be a child molester.

Is an LGBT person someone who was sexually abused as a child?

Although some LGBT people were sexually abused as children, just like their heterosexual counterparts, there is no evidence to suggest that sexual abuse "makes" someone LGBT. We do know that sexual abuse can make a child very confused, and therefore, some youth who have experienced sexual abuse might be categorized as questioning youth.

Are lesbian or gay people the way they are because they have not met the right man or woman?

No. In fact, many gay or lesbian people have been either partnered with or married to opposite-gender individuals. Being lesbian or gay is not a matter of meeting the right person of the opposite gender—again, it is about finding the right internal sense of fit with a person, usually of the same gender.

Couldn't LGBT people really be heterosexual if they tried?

Many LGBT people have tried to be heterosexual. Being LGBT is so condemned by many in our society that many LGBT people try to pretend to be heterosexual, at least for part of their lives. Some try for a lifetime, never acting on or acknowledging their LGBT feelings. Others find ways to adapt to their feelings through furtive relationships, living on the "down low." Some remain married for years but make agreements with their spouses, such as having open marriages. And of course, others still separate or divorce and seek new relationships.

How can you tell if a person is LGBT?

Although at one time many people thought that LGBT people were identifiable through stereotypical mannerisms, affectations, dress, and so on—the only real way to tell if a person is

LGBT is if he or she tells you. There is some slim evidence
(Rule & Ambady, 2008; Rule, Ambady, & Hallett, 2009) in
emerging science where recognition of facial characteristics of
LGBT people is offered as suggestion that perhaps "gaydar"
does exist. The problem with this research from a practice perspective is that looking for "cues" may keep youth workers
from having meaningful open dialogue with youth about issues
pertaining to sexuality, and youth workers may also misread
cues. The ostensible myth of "gaydar" is, in my opinion, an un-
reliable approach for making a determination about someone's
sexual orientation. Too often youth workers continue to look for
the stereotypical gender-nonconforming behaviors or mannerisms, but by and large, LGBT people are a very diverse group,
and come in all colors, cultures, religions, sizes, ages, tempera-
ments, and degrees of masculinity and femininity.

Are LGBTQ people normal?

If normal means "like the majority," then LGBT people aren't.
But, like left-handed people are not in the majority and yet are
viewed as normal, most LGBTQ people believe that their LGBT
sexual or gender orientation is normal. For them to be other-
wise would not be normal.

Is there an LGBTQ culture?

LGBTQ youth come from all cultures, races, ethic backgrounds,
religions, and social classes. Generally, LGBTQ youth adopt the
norms of their particular cultures, races, and classes as adolescents. LGBTQ youth have their own shared language certainly,
but they also have their own personal senses of humor, styles of
dress, social events, and norms.

Because LGBTQ youth culture is very regionalized, it is not
possible to spell out all of the norms, styles, and social events
typical in each area, but youth workers should be attuned to
listen and look carefully within their own areas to determine
the nuances of the subculture there. LGBTQ youth—whether

they live in a rural, suburban, or urban area—probably blend in to the overall adolescent culture as much as any young person does. But there are some unique distinctions as well.

In large urban areas, particularly in the Northeastern part of the United States—New York, Philadelphia, Washington, DC— some LGBTQ youth participate in a social phenomenon known as "the ball scene." Balls are widely advertised and held in large auditoriums or clubs rented especially for the evening. A "house" usually hosts balls. Houses are social clubs headed by a "house mother" and a "house father." Participants from other houses (there are thousands of them—Mizrahi, Extravaganza, Chanel, Latex, Dior) come from all over the city to "walk the ball." Young people walk in whatever category they feel they are best suited for—e.g., best face, best body, best designer labels, realness, and many others categories, some funny and some serious. Trophies are given for the winners, and losers are "chopped," or taken out of competition. The competition is fierce and sometimes not pleasant for those who are deemed as losers. The ball scene is frequented by gay males, young lesbians, transgender youth, and in some cases by heterosexual youth as well.

Many LGBTQ youth use slang terms for one another—gay boys will sometimes jokingly call each other *girl* or *faggot*. Lesbian girls will in a playful way call each other *butch* or *dyke*. In most cases it is not appropriate for adults to use these terms with the youth; they are strictly in-group terms that youth use with each another. Some youth have also reclaimed the term *queer* as an inclusive term, stripping it of its original hurtful intent and transforming it into a very positive word. This is also a generational term; many LGBT adults avoid this term, but many youth claim it as their own.

Is there an LGBT lifestyle?

Many LGBT people object to this term because it trivializes LGBT peoples' lives. If you are LGBT then you have a life, not a lifestyle. Just as there is no such thing as a heterosexual lifestyle, there is no such thing as an LGBT lifestyle.

Do gay men hate women, and do lesbians hate men?

In life there are obvious tensions that exist between the genders—male and female. Some gay men hate women, and some lesbians hate men, just like some heterosexual men hate women and some heterosexual women hate men. But in general, gay men do not hate women, and lesbians do not hate men.

Do LGBT people hate heterosexual people?

Some LGBT people have hostile feelings for heterosexual people, but generally, the answer to this question is no. LGBT people have experienced some terrible things at the hands of heterosexual people, but often LGBT people count many heterosexuals among their friends.

What is heterocentrism?

Heterocentrism is understood as a result of heterosexual privilege and is analogous to racism, sexism, and other ideologies of oppression (Pharr, 1988). Heterocentrism—which I feel most accurately describes the systemic display of LGBT discrimination in major social institutions, in this case the youth-serving systems—has as its primary assumption that the world is and should be heterosexual. This assumption, illustrated most clearly by heterosexual privilege, causes LGBT individuals to engage in a constant balance between their individual natures, which are stigmatized by Western society (and usually by their families), and their environments, which are generally hostile and void of emotional and psychological nutrients necessary for healthy growth. In the case example below, Victor provides a clear illustration of the concept of heterocentrism in a family system.

Victor, a 20-year-old gay Latino, lives in New York City with his father, Manuel, and his 16-year-old sister. Victor's father always reminds him of his responsibility as a man.

When Manuel talks to Victor, he speaks to him about getting married, raising a family, and taking care of his family. Manuel has tried very hard to be a good father, but what he is unaware of is that his son is gay. Although Victor dated a few girls while in high school, he began to understand himself as gay when he was in his freshman year at college. Victor knows his father will have a difficult time accepting his gay identity. At the present time, Victor has decided not to tell him. It makes him sad that his dad has all of these heterosexually oriented dreams for him—dreams that Victor thinks will never be realized.

Why do so many people have trouble accepting LGBT people?

There are many reasons why people, including professionals, have trouble accepting LGBT people, but one primary reason is discomfort with the topic. Sexuality of all types makes many people uncomfortable; same-sex sexuality and transsexuality, however, seem to make people even more uncomfortable.

In addition, since many values in American society come from a Judeo-Christian perspective, many people have difficulty accepting LGBT people from a religious/moral perspective. Working with LGBTQ youth must be, I believe, approached from an amoral perspective—outside of and apart from a personal moral standpoint. Some people are uncomfortable dealing with LGBTQ issues because of their own biases. Through training and self-awareness sessions, staff can find ways to manage their own anxieties and discomfort to practice more effectively.

What should I do if an LGBT person makes a pass at me?

The same thing that you would do if a heterosexual person made a pass at you—if you're not attracted, you say "thanks, but no thanks." If you are interested, you can make your interest known in a variety of ways. Unless of course you are in a client-staff situation, in which case you as the staff member are responsible for ethical behavior, which would preclude any personal, physical, or romantic attachments with a client.

What Can Youth Workers Do?

One of the best ways of preparing to work with LGBTQ youth is to examine your own issues with respect to LGBTQ people. All of us who work with clients walk around with what I call "the big red button" on the top of our heads. That is my visual metaphor for the one (or more) sensitive point that triggers a personally based, emotional reaction. Knowing the issues that set you off—that push your buttons—is crucial to good practice. Although it is not always possible to avoid the emotional issues that upset us when dealing with clients, it is feasible and imperative to develop a sense of mastery over our reactions to the feelings that these sensitive issues trigger. As a professional, openly acknowledging and addressing these issues with a supervisor or a close colleague is a challenge. But also as a professional, it is critical to be self-reflective and to work on development of a professional sense of self, which includes a heightened sense of self-awareness. Allowing personal issues to cloud one's judgment in working with a client is unethical and wrong.

The following is a guide describing first the negative approaches that youth workers may take, and then the positive approaches that lead to exemplary practice. This guide is adapted from Garnets, Hancock, Cochran, Goodchilds, and Peplau (1991).

Guide to Working with LGBTQ Youth

Negative Approaches

Assessment

- believes that LGBT identity is a disorder/pathology
- automatically attributes problems to gender/sexual orientation
- discounts self-disclosure of gender/sexual orientation as a "stage" or "phase"
- fails to recognize heterocentrism or internalized homophobia
- assumes heterosexuality
- acts on the belief that LGBT identity is sinful, or morally wrong

Intervention

- irrelevantly focuses on gender/sexual orientation
- applies pressure to change gender/sexual orientation
- trivializes gender/sexual orientation or experience
- inappropriately transfers client after client's disclosure
- allows personal beliefs to affect quality of interactions and unconditional positive regard of client

Identity

- does not understand LGBTQ identity development
- does not sufficiently take into account effects of internalized homophobia
- underestimates possible consequences of coming out

Relationships and Family

- underestimates importance of intimate relationships
- uses heterosexual frame of reference
- presumes LGBT client to be poor parent
- is insensitive to prejudice toward LGBT families

Youth Worker Expertise and Training

- lacks expertise and relies on client to educate them about issues
- teaches inaccurate information or discriminates against LGBT trainees/colleagues

---

Positive Approaches

Assessment

- understands that LGBT identity does not equal pathology
- recognizes effects of societal heterocentrism
- recognizes gender/sexual orientation is one of many attributes; does not assume it is necessarily relevant to problems
- recognizes the unique concerns of LGBT youth of color
- recognizes issues regarding a sexuality identity or gender identity issues

Intervention

- uses understanding of homophobia to guide therapy
- recognizes effects of own gender/sexual orientation, attitudes, or lack of knowledge
- does not engage in "change therapy" strategies

Identity

- assists in development of positive LGBT identity
- is inclusive of client's strengths related to her or his identity

Relationships and Family

- understands and validates diversity of relationships
- recognizes importance of extended families and created families
- recognizes effect of prejudice and discrimination on relationships and parenting
- recognizes that family of origin may need education and support

Youth Worker Expertise and Training

- knows needs and treatment issues, and can identify community-based resources
- educates trainees/colleagues and actively counters misunderstanding and discrimination

2

The Coming Out Process

Young people who have feelings of attraction for the same gender often become aware of these feelings around the same time that all people become aware of their feelings of attraction. For many people these feelings become strong during adolescence. For heterosexually oriented adolescents, these feelings are reinforced by their families, by society, culture, religion, and peers as a natural part of growing up. Boys are expected to have a girlfriend and girls are expected to have a boyfriend—these are expectations made at very early ages.

For LGBTQ youth, the growing up experience is a very different one. Even before they may be fully aware of how they feel, LGBTQ youth are told that these feelings are not acceptable or normal. Kevin remembers it this way:

> I remember at about age 5 or so, saying that I liked dolls and my father became so angry with me. He started to say that boys play with trucks, dolls were for girls. He seemed so mad about me saying this, which I just never said it again, but the feelings never went away. In fact, when I became about 13 or so, these feelings grew stronger. I didn't have a name for what I felt, but I knew that I was "different" somehow. I had brothers and I knew what they liked

and didn't like and when I compared myself to them, I
knew that I was different from them. My clearest memory
is when I was watching the TV show *Batman* after school
one day and I looked at Robin's legs in those tights and I
thought to myself—"Oh, my, he is so cute!" I knew other
boys weren't thinking like that—they were trying to imi-
tate Batman and Robin's fighting moves, you remember,
"pow!", "smash!"—but I was admiring Robin's muscular
legs. I knew other boys were not doing that. That's when I
first started to figure things out.

This feeling of "differentness" is fairly common for many
LGBTQ youth—but not all. Hearing other kids or family members use hurtful names about LGBTQ youth can reinforce the
negative images that youth may have about themselves. Because of negative reinforcement, most LGBTQ youth hide their
gender/sexual orientation and pretend to be heterosexual.

Hiding and Invisibility

Nina is a 16-year-old Caucasian lesbian. She lives at home
with her mother, who is a single parent, and her two
younger brothers, ages 8 and 13. Nina has always known
that she was "different." When she was 5 or 6 she was
called a tomboy by everyone. They all said that she would
grow out of it, they told her it was "just a phase"—but by
the time she was 13, she knew they were wrong. She liked
girls "that way." It took her a while to accept herself as a
lesbian, because of all the terrible things people always
said about lesbians. She is not open about her sexual orientation with her mother because she is afraid of her reaction. She knows a couple of girls in school who identify as
bisexual, but she is very careful about who she tells. Sometimes, Nina feels very stressed, because it's not easy to
keep something that is so much a part of herself a secret.

Since there are no outward features to identify an LGBTQ young person like Nina in the above vignette, most LGBTQ young people are invisible to their families, their friends, and many youth service providers (see DeCrescenzo, 1994; Savin-Williams, 2001, 2006). Invisibility is one of the most dominant features of an LGBTQ young person's identity. Invisibility makes it difficult for service providers to know who to provide services to. But LGBTQ youth are invisible for many reasons:

- Fear of rejection from friends and family members
- Fear of verbal harassment
- Fear of physical violence
- Fear of being treated differently
- Fear of being misunderstood
- Fear of being completely sexualized
- Fear of being perceived as sick, deviant, or sinful

It is important to understand the reasons why LGBTQ youth are invisible and to understand the process by which they are socialized to hide their gender/sexual orientation from others. Some youth, like Nina in the example above, repress their feelings—waiting until later to act on them, pushing them down—and monitor their behavior, speech, or styles of dress. Such self-monitoring can cause many LGBTQ youth to experience stresses that are devastating to their mental health and physical well-being. Other LGBTQ youth sublimate their feelings in either positive or negative ways. Positive acts can include over-involvement in sports, academics, extracurricular activities, or church groups. They try to be the best little boy or best little girl in the world to cover over the part of themselves that they feel is very bad. Negative acts include abuse of substances, putting oneself in dangerous situations, and having "accidents."

Such methods may be useful for a while, but the stress of sublimation does not permit the adolescent to live life fully, and his or her development is truncated. Some LGBTQ people successfully hide until adulthood. Some marry, have children, even grandchildren, and then come out at age 65. Some LGBTQ people hide their entire lives, using substances or work or food to cover their secret. Other LGBTQ people, thankfully, accept their identity as an LGBTQ person and come out.

Coming out is a distinctly LGBTQ phenomenon. It is something that non-LGBTQ youth do not have to deal with. Coming out is a process, not a one-time event, and it is a personal decision for each person who struggles with gender or sexual identity issues. Living in the closet is exhausting and scary. Watching everything that they do and say is the hardest thing that many LGBTQ youth have to do. Many LGBTQ work hard to keep their secret—some become experts at hiding, but at great expense to their health and well-being.

Being found out, which is different than coming out in that it is an unplanned disclosure, refers to a situation when a person does not have an option about coming out and they unexpectedly get found out. When this happens in a family, in most cases a crisis situation results. The following vignette is an example of this phenomenon:

> I came home from school one day and found my mother crying at the kitchen table. I was so upset when I saw her that I ran to her and said, "Mommie, what's the matter? What happened?" She didn't say anything; she just handed me this letter that a boy who I liked in school had written to me, and it was the kind of letter that most boys do not write to one another. I had it hidden, I thought, in my dresser, but I guess she found it when she was straightening up. When I saw that letter, my heart just sank. I knew that things would never again be the same. Now she knew—I wasn't ready to tell her, but she knew.

Being found out throws the entire family system—not just the LGBTQ youth—into a crisis, and most families will need assistance to emerge intact from this crisis state. It is essential that youth workers have an adequate grasp of LGBTQ identity issues before a crisis occurs, as they might be the person called upon to assist the youth and his or her family in dealing with the issues of being found out.

If a young person is found out by his or her family, the family will need support, assistance, and compassionate understanding from those trying to help them. Youth workers will need to know of services in the community where family members can find this support or be prepared to provide it themselves.

In cases where youth workers will have to provide the support, they will need to be prepared to provide an array of services to both the youth affected and his or her family. They might be called upon to provide written information to both youth and family members about gender/sexual orientation issues. They might also have to utilize some crisis intervention strategies for families who are more prone to verbal abuse or physical confrontations. Youth workers might need to find a respite situation (temporary safe housing) or find permanent shelter placement for a youth that has been thrown out of his or her home.

Stigma

Because LGBTQ youth are stigmatized, and because many adults view youth through a lens of heterosexuality, an understanding of stigma is important for youth workers to grasp.

In this context, *stigma* is defined as a metaphorical blot on one's identity, and it is one factor that makes LGBTQ youth different from their heterosexual counterparts. LGBTQ youth live with the knowledge that their identity as an LGBTQ person is stigmatized and despised by society. Although many LGBTQ people have gained acceptance from the mainstream culture, some people still view an LGBTQ identity as a stigmatizing status, something to hide, or to be ashamed of. If this were not so, virtually everyone who was LGBTQ would be out and open about their gender/sexual orientation.

LGBTQ youth of color are dealing with possible oppression on multiple levels and therefore may have additional stresses associated with coming out (Walters & Old Person, 2008).

Why is it important to tell people that you are LGBT?

Although LGBT people tell their families and friends that they are gay for many reasons, they primarily do it because they want to be free to be themselves. They want to be honest with those that they trust and love. It is also exhausting and personally destructive to pretend to be someone who you are not.

Some LGBT people come out gradually, telling the most important people in their lives first, usually friends. Many continue the coming out process by then gradually telling others—family, coworkers, etc. Coming out, however, is a continual process for people; once LGBT people refuse to hide or masquerade as heterosexual, the opportunities for disclosure are many.

Coming out, especially for LGBTQ youth, is a very liberating experience. It is like being free after a long imprisonment. Some youth, not yet secure with their newly accepted identity, can go to extremes by dressing differently or acting differently—as some people might say, *flaunting* their identity.

Flaunting It

Like their heterosexual counterparts, LGBTQ youth have no desire to make a spectacle of themselves, but they do want to be able to be themselves. What is generally attributed to flaunting one's LGBTQ identity is usually an adaptation to living life openly as an LGBTQ person. The discomfort that some observers feel is their unfamiliarity with LGBTQ people being open about their sexual or gender orientation.

What Can Youth Workers Do?

The only sure way of identifying an LGBTQ youth is when he or she self-discloses his or her orientation to you—in other words, when he or she comes out to you. It is important to remember that the goal of youth work with a possible LGBTQ youth is not to get them to come out to you, but to facilitate the experience of coming out, if and when a young person decides it is all right to do so. Facilitating the experience means that youth workers need to do the following:

- Use the words gay, lesbian, bisexual, transgender, and questioning. Using these words and being able to say them with comfort suggests that you are all right with these issues, and possibly, that you are a person it's okay to talk with about these issues.
- Rather than looking for the LGBTQ "cues" in the youth, send out your own cues that say loudly and clearly that you are comfortable discussing issues of gender/sexual orientation.
- Make sure that your workplace has some visible signs that it is all right to be an LGBTQ youth in your program— posters, books, and flyers around the office are all very useful and clear signs.
- Do not make or tolerate jokes or negative comments about anyone based on race, culture, national origin, gender, ability, age, religion, or gender/sexual orientation—and be clear about why.
- Provide all young people with opportunities to talk about gender and sexuality in a healthy way and be sure to include LGBTQ people in those discussions.
- Help your organization respond to the needs of LGBTQ youth by encouraging training, organizational reform, and review of policies that might discriminate against LGBTQ youth.
- Realize that LGBTQ youth have more to their identities than the fact that they are gay, lesbian, bisexual, transgender, or questioning. They are just like other young people who need support, appropriate adult role models, care, concern, guidance, and flexibility.

In their training curriculum, Elze and McHaelen (2009, p. 78) offer some useful suggestions that focus on what to do after a youth discloses his or her gender/sexual orientation to a worker. Some of these suggestions have been summarized here below:

- Youth workers should be prepared to affirm, validate, and accept youths' expressions of same-gender attractions, desires, and behaviors; gender variance; and self-identification.
- Utilizing a good social work principle of practice, youth workers should remember to start where the client is and proceed with gentleness and patience.
- Youth workers should stay away from labeling, but instead help youth safely explore their feelings, thoughts, and behaviors related to sexuality and gender identity.
- It is important to remember that sexual orientation and gender identity are different constructs. Transgender youth may self-identify as gay, lesbian, bisexual, or heterosexual, or they may be questioning their sexual orientation or not labeling themselves. Youth workers should focus on validating the youth's sexual orientation as it unfolds. Transgender youth may need additional help in differentiating between their gender identity and sexual orientation.
- Allow the young person to take the lead in using whatever terminology he or she feels comfortable using. However, it is important that the youth worker is able to say the words *gay, lesbian, bisexual,* and *transgender* comfortably and without hesitation.
- When a youth discloses to a youth worker that she or he is LGBTQ, workers need to respond in an affirming, supportive way; anticipate concerns about confidentiality; and give the message that they are willing to talk about any issue.

When youth come out, they are disclosing very personal information about themselves that could potentially lead to negative outcomes in their lives; violence and isolation may also be a fear. Make sure to help them examine their fears of coming out. Discuss the possible anticipated consequences.

Youth workers should anticipate LGBTQ youths' feelings of vulnerability. Be aware that a youth's disclosure to you makes him or her highly vulnerable, because you as a youth worker have the power to tell others. The youth may be afraid that you will not protect his or her identity.

As a youth worker, you are in a position of authority over LGBTQ youth. They are very aware that they lack control in this aspect of their lives. Be sure to acknowledge their trust in you. Make sure you discuss confidentiality and what that means for you and for them.

- It is also important to know that not all LGBTQ youth will be clear or comfortable about their emerging gender or sexual orientation when they first come out. Some youth may be distressed and others may be confused about their feelings. Youth workers should be prepared to encourage further expression of feelings, worries, and concerns; to explore with them their underlying beliefs and attitudes; and to correct any misinformation about LGBTQ issues or identity.

It is equally important for youth workers to be able to validate the youths' confusion. Let young people who are confused know it is normal to be confused, and explore their confusion with them. Youth workers should be prepared to be affirming and supportive, and able to assess the youth's level of information and provide accurate information, correcting myths and stereotypes as they come up. Youth workers should be very careful not to push youth toward premature resolution of sexual and/or gender identity.

Young people who have been sexually abused may require even more time to work out their sexual identity. Sometimes, experiencing sexual abuse can cause confusion about sexual orientation—this important topic will be discussed more fully in Chapter 11, in the section on questioning youth.

Responsibilities of Youth Workers in the Disclosing Process

If a young person discloses to me, should I share it with my coworkers?

In most cases, I would say that you should not share this information with coworkers, but it depends. It depends on whether you share all information about youth in your program with coworkers. It also depends on how comfortable your coworkers are with issues of gender/sexual orientation, and whether you agreed not to disclose this information to anyone.

In some cases, youth should be encouraged to disclose to others when they feel safe and comfortable disclosing to others. But no one, including a youth worker, should ever disclose someone's sexual orientation to anyone without his or her permission. Disclosure is a very personal choice.

Should any of the disclosure/coming out process be documented?

Again, I would say that this depends. It depends on the agreement that a worker makes with a youth when they disclose, and it also depends on the guidelines set by agencies with respect to documentation of sensitive information.

Should I maintain confidentiality?

Confidentiality should also be maintained. No one, including youth workers, should ever take it upon himself or herself to "out" another person. As with other case-sensitive information, without the client's permission, the worker should keep the information confidential.

The Coming Out Process

Stages of Development

The following information is derived from the works of Alan K. Malyon (1982), Vivienne C. Cass (1979, 1984), and Richard R. Troiden (1979, 1993). The stages are offered to provide a baseline of gender/sexual identity development and an understanding of stages a person may encounter during his or her development. As with all human behavior, many factors influence this development and most people do not go through orderly stages. Defining stages of human behavior provides only a base of understanding. Movement from stage to stage is not limited to forward growth. Life experiences influence the movements among the stages. With each stage are suggested action items that can be used in working with young people.

Stage 1: Could I be gay, lesbian, bi, or trans?

Confused about his or her self-image, the young person seeks more information on his or her identity. Some theorists believe this is normal development for all youth. Due to negative reinforcements, more confusion about the self-image is created and the person sees no similarity between the self and the public images of LGBT people.

Action: Encourage the youth to explore his or her feelings, and identify places he or she can get accurate information on LGBTQ identity.

Stage 2: I might be LGBT

When the young person accepts the possibility, he or she may experience alienation, isolation, and loneliness. Previously learned heterosexual behavior has little or no significance. Youth cling to heterosexual behavior to maintain a public image and because they do not have access to alternative gender/sexuality identity role models.

Action: Provide accurate information, and stress that LGBTQ identity can be a positive option. Offer the youth nonerotic novels with LGBT characters, or recommend other opportunities to find positive LGBT role models, including film and television, history, or sports.

Stage 3: I probably am LGBT

Alienation is peaking. The person is driven to seek out other LGBTQ people in the broader culture. The highest priority is that of finding a role model, someone to gauge themselves by. At this stage a positive role model can lead to a positive self-image; a negative role model or lack of role models can lead to self-hatred or further alienation.

Action: Identify and provide access to positive LGBT role models and/or a support/education group.

Stage 4: I am an LGBT person

Acceptance of his or her LGBT identity may lead to experimentation. The person is concerned more about whether he or she fits in to the LGBT subculture than fitting in to the whole culture. This is sometimes difficult for youth. If there is no obvious place for him or her in the subculture, a youth may temporarily end gender/sexual identity formation and enter biphasal development—that is, some youth will live a public heterosexual life but privately engage in or fantasize about LGBT behavior.

Action: To circumvent this cessation of identity formation, one can provide direct access to youth organizations in the LGBT community or service providers. Help the youth identify ways to come out that will build self-esteem. Identify strategies for coping with negative social reactions. Work with adults involved in the youth's community to build an understanding of why the disclosure of the youth's sexual identity is important. In some cases, a youth might be exhibiting all of these behaviors, but still avoids actually coming out, and workers should remember it is not their responsibility to force the youth to come out, but to facilitate the process should the youth wish to at any given point in the future. Youths who exhibit all the behaviors of LGBTQ youth but refuse to come out may be at greater risk for engaging in high-risk and self-abusing behaviors. Although workers should be empathetic and accepting, this will undoubtedly be a difficult time for this sort of youth.

Stage 5: I am lesbian, gay, bisexual, or trans—so what?

Here the person no longer sees a clear dichotomy between heterosexual and LGBT worlds. The person is able to integrate LGBT identity into all aspects of life. This stage assumes a level of maturity and a wide range of life experiences.

Action: Many youth generally haven't achieved this stage. It is helpful to keep this stage in mind as a goal to achieve. Once it is achieved, celebrate!

3

Family Issues

Despite the great strides forward that LGBTQ people have made during the last three decades, one of the hardest things for most LGBTQ youth is coming out to their families.

Families provide for youth economically, emotionally, and socially. They are incredibly important forces in a young person's life. How parents react to an LGBTQ son or daughter probably has a lot to do with who the parents are. In talking here about parents, I am including birth parents and adoptive/foster parents.

Much depends on the family's culture, their backgrounds, the communities that they come from, their racial group, and whether they are deeply religious. Regardless of how open-minded parents are—even if they have LGBT friends, even if they are involved in civil rights issues—many parents are universally upset when they find out that their son or daughter is LGBT. Most parents are completely unprepared for having a child who identifies as gay or lesbian. Bisexual and transgender youth face even more profound issues.

Most parents have a range of reactions, including shock, fear, guilt, shame, denial, disappointment, and sometimes anger and hostility. Many parents, relying on what they have been erroneously told, may hope that their child's disclosure is just a

phase. Others will wonder, "Did I do something wrong?" Some
may express fear about AIDS, worry that they will never have
grandchildren, or think that this is an attempt to punish them in
some way. These reactions may have nothing to do with reality,
but many parents will react based on stereotypes and myths
about LGBTQ people. Youth workers should become familiar
with accurate resources for parents—it is very helpful for parents to know that their child is not the only LBGTQ child. Resources by Bernstein (2003); Fairchild & Hayward (1998);
Griffin, Wirth, & Wirth (1997); and McDougall (2007) are all
excellent resources on parenting an LGBTQ young person.

Foster/Adoptive Parents

Although the range of issues faced by foster/adoptive parents
are similar to those with family of origin, there are some unique
circumstances for LGBTQ youth living with foster/adoptive
families. Foster/adoptive parents who react negatively to a
youth who discloses his or her gender or sexual orientation will
need the same kinds of supports (family counseling, support
groups, access to services) as birth parents to address the disclosure—which may, at least initially, seem like a family crisis.

Foster/adoptive parents need training from the agency about
adolescent sexuality issues, including issues about raising an
LGBTQ youth. All foster/adoptive parents need this type of
training, not just those parents who may already be caring for an
LGBTQ youth. In the absences of this type of education, some
foster/adoptive parents may react negatively to finding out that a
youth in their care is LGBTQ (see Elze & McHaelen, 2009;
Wilber, Ryan, & Markamer, 2006). Some foster/adoptive parents
may express hostile feelings toward the idea of fostering or
adopting an LGBTQ youth—in such cases, agencies need clear
policies to guide these situations. A worker may assume that
placement in such a situation would be uncomfortable and in
most cases unhealthy for an LGBTQ youth. Youth workers
should also be prepared to react to prejudice or hatred directed
at them because of an agency's policies. Such preparation is

even more necessary for youth workers who are openly LGBT themselves. At a minimum, youth workers should expect that their agency will fully support them in these difficult situations.

> Tracey is a 17-year-old male-bodied teen. Since age 6, Tracey has always known that she was a girl, not a boy. She lived in a foster home, with a foster mother and two foster brothers. Her gender identity was ambiguous and her birth name was gender neutral already—but the family saw her as a boy, which is what they were told when Tracey was placed with them. She felt confident that they accepted her as she was, but never felt comfortable talking with them directly about her gender identity.
>
> One day after thinking about how and if she could disclose her gender identity to them, she decided to take a risk and tell them. Tracey sat everyone down at the kitchen table and said, "I know that I have been kinda unclear about who I am with all of you. But I am tired of not being able to be myself. I see myself as a girl, not a boy." At first the family, especially the mother, seemed stunned. But after asking some questions—about when Tracey first knew, and if she felt okay with who she was—the family seemed accepting of her. Tracey felt relieved and her life with her family continued as it had before, but she felt more comfortable with who she was.

Many parents may initially believe that their LGBTQ child needs therapy. Although some LGBTQ young people might need therapy, others may not. It is an initial response, however, for many parents to immediately urge the young person toward therapy. After coming out to his or her parents, especially if there will be more discussion with others, a young person has important considerations about confidentiality: who else should know, how the disclosure should be handled.

Some parents, although upset at the disclosure that their child is LGBT, manage to deal with it in a loving way. Tracey's mother, after being reassured that she was all right and that she was comfortable with her trans identity, was able to talk with her and ask her questions. It also helped that she included her brothers, because now the entire family knew and they could all talk openly about the fact that Tracey was transgender.

Other parents react harshly to a child's disclosure, as in Marianne's case.

> Marianne is a 16-year-old Trinidadian lesbian. Until she came out to her family, she lived with her mother and three sisters in an apartment in Central Toronto. Marianne decided not to tell her mother that she was gay because she was, as Marianne put it, "totally into the church and I knew that she would never deal with me being gay." One evening while Marianne was talking to her girlfriend on the phone, unbeknownst to Marianne, her mother listened in on the extension to their entire conversation. After Marianne hung up her mother confronted her: "Why was that girl talking to you like most girls would talk to a boyfriend?" Marianne tried to play it off and to be cool, but her mother persisted: "Are you gay?" Marianne did not know how to react—but her mother didn't give her a chance to think as she grabbed her by the arm and threw her out of the house, screaming "You are no longer my daughter, I will not have this in my house, you will not do this to me or to your sisters." Marianne was totally unprepared for coming out, never mind being thrown out. She recalled: "All I could think of was 'Oh great, now my mother knows that I'm a lesbian, and I have nowhere to live!'"

LGBTQ youth who are thrown out of their homes are often the most at risk. Many of these young people end up living with friends, in a transitional living program, or in a child welfare residential placement. Several studies from Los Angeles, New York, and Seattle (Kruks, 1991; Mallon, 1998b; Seattle Commission on Children and Youth, 1988) have concluded that LGBTQ youth are overrepresented in the runaway and homeless youth populations and programs that serve them. The

unique issues that confront LGBTQ youth in residential placements will be discussed in Chapter 9, and homeless and runaway youth are highlighted in Chapter 11.

What is often hardest for the parents of an LGBTQ child is
coping with the sense of embarrassment and shame of what
friends, family members, or even strangers will think if they
find out. In one sense, once the LGBTQ youth comes out, in
many cases it is the parents who then find themselves in their
own closet, hiding the truth about their LGBT child. Over
time they are faced with "Does your daughter have a boyfriend?" or "Is your son dating anyone?" and parents have to
decide what to say.

Mothers and Fathers

Although there is some evidence which suggests that women
tend to be more open minded about gender/sexual orientation
issues than men, there is not enough evidence to generalize
that fathers always have more trouble with their gay sons or
mothers always have more trouble with their lesbian daughters.
It is probably safe to say, however, that mothers and fathers
have different expectations for their children depending on
whether their child is a girl or a boy. Mario in the vignette below illuminates some of these expectations:

> We're Italian, my family, and so when I came out to my fa-
> ther, he flipped. He started saying, "You're a man. I raised
> you to be a man. What happened? Did I do something
> wrong? Didn't I take you to Little League, Midget Foot-
> ball? I can't believe this!" Somehow he equated being gay
> to being less of a man. He got over it after a while—but I'll
> never forget his first reaction.

Families of color have other issues with a child who comes
out as LGBT. Many families believe that dealing with an oppressed status such as skin color is enough. One young African
American lesbian from New York put it this way:

I told my grandmother that I was gonna come out and she said "Girl, you better go right back in. You are not coming out in this house—we got enough to deal with already."

Grandparents

"Whatever you do, don't tell your grandmother, it would kill her, and you're her favorite. She'll never need to know." These kinds of admonishments are frequently heard from well-intentioned family members. The truth is that many grandparents are much more accepting of what their grandchildren do than they are of what their own children do. Grandparents also have family history and knowledge on their side. One young person told me this story about telling his grandmother that he was gay:

After I told her she said, "Oh, you know you're not the first family member who is gay." I was shocked, I couldn't even think of who she meant, and then she said, "Remember your Aunt Libby and Aunt Pearl? Well, Aunt Pearl was your grandfather's sister, and Aunt Libby was her lady friend. Although we never really spoke about it, they were gay." I couldn't believe what I was hearing. But it made me feel much better to know I wasn't the first.

Brothers and Sisters

Like parents and grandparents, siblings react in a variety of ways toward an LGBTQ sibling's disclosure. Some are supportive, some are not. Some siblings may be fearful that their friends might think that they are also gay. Others will become advocates and champions of LGBTQ causes. One young woman made this reflection about her sister's reaction to her coming out:

One day my sister was really angry with me and I couldn't figure out why. When I confronted her she finally said, "You know, I know that you are very proud of being a lesbian, but I am not proud of it. You just keep coming out all

Family Issues   63

over the place and then I start getting all of these looks in
the hallway from everyone." I never realized what an impact my coming out had on my sister. I realized that I had
to be more sensitive to her wishes as well.

What Can Youth Workers Do?

There are many things that youth workers can do to assist both
the family and the young person in this process. Primarily,
youth workers can be aware of the stages of coming out for
families. Griffin et al. (1997) suggest that there are several
steps that many families may go through in dealing with a son
or daughter's disclosure of an LGBT identity.

1. The first step is that families find out that their child is
    LGBT. When they find out, families have many emotional
    reactions. In some cases families might cut off contact with
    the young person; some youth may even be thrown out of
    their homes. In other cases, families might pursue conver-
    sion strategies—they might try through therapy or other
    means to change their family member's orientation. Other
    families still might just shut down and enter a phase of de-
    nial about their loved one's sexual/gender orientation. Fi-
    nally, some families might openly acknowledge and accept
    the gender or sexual orientation of their family member.
2. When one member of the family comes out, the entire fami-
    ly comes out. As such, communicating with others about
    their family members' gender or sexual orientation becomes
    the second step in this process. Some families may feel
    comfortable and begin to tell select friends about their fam-
    ily member. Family members in this phase will see that
    there is a great deal of learning from LGBTQ children and
    other LGBT people that can take place. Other families will
    learn from counselors and some might benefit from peer
    support by attending parents' groups and thereby learning
    from other parents of LGBT children.
3. Families will need to move toward changing their inner
    perceptions about LGBT people. Those families who are

willing may open up a whole range of feelings, including grief, guilt, anger, failure, sadness, shame, loneliness, and fear. As families move toward acceptance they will undoubtedly address these feelings and others.

4. Finally, developing a level of comfort in telling others about their family member's gender or sexual orientation may involve confronting homophobic comments from society, from friends, or from other family members. Family members may realize that in their own ways and in their own time, they must come out as parents. Some parents might begin to speak up and out in public; others may openly educate critics; many will find comfort in allying with other parents of LGBTQ youth.

There are as well some positive reactions identified by Ryan, Huebner, Diaz, & Sanchez (2009) that families may feel in relation to their LGBTQ family member. Some of these are: pride, respect, affection, validation, confirmation of earlier perceptions that their child might be LGBT, admiration for the child's capacity to be a role model for others, supportive interest, and excitement for the child's future as an LGBT adult.

Youth workers should remember that on average, LGBTQ youth have been thinking about their sexual orientation for approximately two years before they tell their parents.

Helping the Young Person Decide

The following suggestions are designed to assist youth workers in developing sensitivity toward youth who are debating whether they should come out to their families.

1. Not all young people should be encouraged to disclose to their families. In some cases, disclosure is not advisable. First determine why the youth has decided to disclose at this point in time and help him or her to figure out the consequences of this disclosure (see point #12).

2. Ask the young person if there are any other family members who are LGBTQ.

3. Talk with the young person about their age at coming out,

about racial and cultural issues, and about geographic issues. Youth living in urban, rural, and suburban environments may have many different experiences based on locale, as might younger and older teens.

4. The youth worker should explore how open or how closed the family system has generally been to new ideas and new people.

5. The youth worker should ask how the family system has dealt with new and unexpected information historically. Such questions can provide insight into the family's flexibility and may assist in determining which family members will be supportive and which will not.

6. The youth worker should ask the client a series of questions such as: Who do you feel most close to? Who have you confided in and who has confided in you? Who do you perceive to be the most liberal members of the family and who will handle this information best? And how does the family grapevine work? Such exploration might help the individual decide who might be the most supportive family member to disclose to initially, if he or she does disclose. Genograms and eco-maps may also be useful tools in this process, by helping the individual to graphically depict family systems. These tools allow for matter-of-fact questioning which can assist in gathering sensitive information.

7. Youth workers should be available to role-play the disclosure process with clients. They should explore with the client several perspectives and offer feedback and suggestions on how the transaction can be accomplished more smoothly.

8. Youth workers should help clients to see that coming out to family members is not a one-time situation, but a process. As individuals and their families disclose on a continuum, clients should be encouraged to consider first disclosing to a family member with whom they are emotionally closest.

9. Youth workers should assist clients in developing a plan for orchestrating the disclosure to the family.

10. Youth workers should be available to support and meet with parents and other family members. At the outset, this

situation usually requires crisis intervention strategies. At the point of being "found out" or the point at which the young person "comes out," parents themselves are usually so needy for emotional support that they might be unavailable to parent the young person. Therefore, the time immediately following the confirmation that their child is LGBTQ is when parents require the greatest amount of nurturing and support from both their child and the youth worker. Siblings will also need assistance during this time and should not be neglected in the process. Encouraging them to explore feelings, providing them with educational information, and making them aware of support groups for families such as Parents and Friends of Lesbians and Gays (PFLAG) is an important part of this process. Knowledge about local family-based resources in the community is also essential.

11. Youth workers should remain available to assist both the family and the individual in negotiating this process.

12. Youth workers should also be able to appraise when it is not advisable for a young person to come out to his or her family.

13. Religious leaders may also be consulted to advise on these matters. Youth workers should have access to members of the clergy from various faiths in the community.

14. Explaining that they are not the cause of their child's LGBT gender/sexual orientation can help parents.

15. Family members need support in going through their own "coming out" process—see the four-step description on page 52–55.

16. Youth workers must realize that coming out will be a long-term process and that both the youth and his or her family may need to meet and discuss these issues several times more in the future.

4

Discrimination and Anti-LGBTQ Harassment and Violence

Many LGBT researchers have suggested that the primary task of identity development for an LGBTQ youth is to learn to manage a stigmatized identity. Unlike their heterosexual counterparts—who are members of the dominant culture—LGBTQ youth, as sexual minorities, must learn to manage their gender or sexual identity. Identity management essentially means: who do you decide to tell that you are LGBT, and who don't you tell? Although negative attitudes toward LGBTQ youth are slowly changing, discrimination in the lives of LGBTQ youth still exists.

Discrimination

Although LGBTQ people are protected by legislation in several states, many LGBTQ youth report experiencing discrimination in schools, in foster care placements, in employment, and in the military. Discrimination is not always blatant, but most often comes in cloaked insidious ways—the vacancy becomes filled in the group home when they hear that the youth is gay, the school is concerned with its dress code when a young lesbian dresses "too butch," the job becomes unavailable when the applicant is "discovered" to be a transgender individual.

LGBTQ youth of color are at even greater risk for discrimination, on multiple levels. To assist in protecting LGBTQ youth from discrimination, several national organizations—among them the National Organization of Social Workers, the American Psychological Association, and the American Psychiatric Association—have drafted statements about their policies on LGBTQ issues. It is the role of youth workers to act as an advocate for equity, fair treatment, and justice when LGBTQ youth are discriminated against. Although advocacy is not always an easy role for youth workers, it is an essential one for those concerned with the health and well-being of all youth.

Anti-LGBTQ Harassment and Violence

LGBTQ young people, unlike their heterosexual counterparts, are targeted for attack specifically because of their gender/ sexual orientation. North American culture—pervaded by a heterocentric ideological system that denies, denigrates, and stigmatizes LGBTQ people—simultaneously makes LGBTQ individuals invisible and legitimizes hostility, discrimination, and even violence against them. Safety has always been an issue for LGBTQ individuals. LGBTQ youth must assess issues of safety in their lives on a daily basis. When LGBTQ young people engage in behaviors allowed for heterosexual young people (such as walking down a street holding hands or kissing), they make public what Western society has prescribed as private. They are accused of flaunting their sexuality and are thereby perceived as deserving of or even asking for retribution, harassment, or assault.

It should be no surprise then that LGBTQ youth in various studies report high frequency of verbal harassment and physical violence directed toward them because of their sexual orientation. In one study that I conducted with LGBTQ youth in child welfare settings in New York, Los Angeles, and Toronto, (Mallon, 1998b) more than 70% of the participants reported being victims of physical violence because of their sexual orientation, and more than 90% reported verbal harassment.

When asked about verbal harassment, one youth in the study reported:

> The name-calling was just a given, I almost didn't even think to mention that because it always happened. The verbal harassment was regular.

There were reports of violence also within family systems, in schools, and in the community. Tirades from family members, peers, and in some cases staff members began with taunts and name-calling and sometimes escalated into physical violence: punches, burnings, and rape. One worker reported an incident of community violence:

> This one young boy was taunted and teased so badly in the community that he couldn't even go outside, the kids would chase him. There was an incident where this guy in the neighborhood molested him, it was just horrible, it was just very, very bad and we had a lot of difficulty in the community. I mean, this child just couldn't even live in the community in peace. We eventually had to move him for his own safety.

LGBTQ young people are often deemed disposable individuals, deserving of being jostled into line or kept in the closet. Many have frequently found youth-oriented environments to be so poor of a fit for them that they felt as though they literally had to flee for their lives. The stigma attached to being LGBTQ often prevents youth from reporting their victimization. Many young people reported that when the abuse was acknowledged, the victims themselves were blamed. Consequently, more than half of the young people who were informants in my study (Mallon, 1998b) at some point in time chose the apparent safety of the streets over the foster care system.

Identity management is closely linked to safety issues. If youth believe that they might be at risk for verbal harassment or physical violence if they come out or get found out, they will probably hide if they can.

Youth who are perceived to be LGBTQ are equally at risk for verbal harassment or violence. The perception alone that one is gay, lesbian, bisexual, or transgender may be sufficient to provoke a violent reaction. Therefore, youth workers must also be aware of the dangers for youth who are perceived to be LGBTQ. Since some people react in a hostile way toward youth who are or are perceived to be LGBTQ—as evidenced in the following vignette—safety is a huge issue for youth workers to grapple with.

Harry is a 16-year-old African American youth. Since grade school, Harry has been seen by his peers as gay but he identifies as heterosexual. He is not, in his words, "in the closet"—he clearly identifies as straight. Harry has been the target of teasing and bullying all of his life. The situation seems particularly intolerable when he is in a new situation. When he first entered high school he was assaulted by two other youth who accosted him on the street after basketball practice, hurling antigay epithets at him and jumping him. Since that time, Harry makes sure not to walk home without a friend.

Although some professionals might suggest that not disclosing one's orientation might be the practical solution, this is clearly not the best resolution to this issue. As evidenced by Harry's story, perception alone is sometimes enough to trigger a violent reaction. This suggestion also puts the burden of responsibility on the LGBTQ youth and not on those who are engaged in the verbal harassment or the violent acts.

What Can Youth Workers Do?

Professionals faced with these harsh realities might ask what can be done. This inquiry is the reminder that all youth work professionals have the ethical and moral responsibility to create and maintain safe environments for *every* young person in their care. The foundation of this safety is at the very core of all youth development practice.

- Open a dialogue with all youth, not just LGBTQ youth, about dealing with and accepting diversity. Have open discussions with all youth about diversity in sexual orientation.
- Include content on gay, lesbian, bisexual, and transgender experiences when discussing human sexuality with all youth.
- Develop an antislur policy that protects all racial, cultural, religious, or sexual orientation groups.
- Have a zero tolerance policy for all forms of violence.
- Post a list of rules and regulations that clearly state that all people regardless of race, religion, sexual orientation, culture, gender, and ability are respected and celebrated.
- Have discussions about gender appropriate behaviors and mannerisms and why they do not indicate one's sexual orientation.
- Make sure that your organization has discussions about the negative effects that discrimination and violence has for all youth.
- Make sure that adults model appropriate accepting behaviors for youth.
- Staff should be accountable in the supervision and evaluation processes for their demonstrated skills in creating a safe environment and for unconditional acceptance.

5

Creating Healthy and Affirming Social Environments

All youth deserve support and an environment in which they are free to learn and free to socialize with peers without fear of harassment or violence. Safe, supportive environments are essential for young people who are LGBTQ.

Although LGBTQ youth do not always require special services designed for them, they do require services that are responsive to their needs. LGBTQ and non-gay youth can and should be integrated into existing youth services, but there are circumstances when specific LGBTQ-affirming services should be created. Youth workers should stay up-to-date on current law and business policy that bans discrimination. Workers may also use current events as a springboard for discussion about impacts on the community.

Determining Safety

LGBTQ youth become experts at determining whether their immediate environment is a safe one. They have to because so much depends on it. LGBTQ people learn to scan their environment to determine whether it is a safe environment for them to be open about their sexual orientation. LGBTQ youth are by definition outsiders, outside the norm, different. No matter how

integrated an LGBTQ youth is into his or her family, community, or school, he or she is still not part of the majority. LGBTQ
youth are frequently fearful of being judged or discriminated
against because they are LGBTQ.

Historically, LGBTQ youth have had to struggle to find their
community. As they are beginning to explore their identities,
many of these youth believe that they are the only ones who
feel as they do. Living in such a state of isolation can cause a
young person to become depressed, anxious, and sad. At some
point when LGBTQ youth begin to realize that they are not the
only LGBTQ people in the world, they have a strong desire to
find others "like them," as this young person reported:

> Before I came out I really and truly believed that I was the
> only guy who liked other guys. There was no one in my
> school who I could tell was gay and I certainly didn't know
> any adults who were gay—I felt so lonely. On top of every-
> thing, I couldn't talk to anybody about how I felt, not my
> friends, my family, anyone. When I finally figured out that
> there were others who were like me—I read this book called
> *Young, Gay and Proud* [Alyson, 1991], I couldn't wait to find
> them. But I had no idea where to begin looking for my kind.

Since LGBTQ youth may have limited information about
their own emerging identity, many embark on a quest to find
"their kind." Until the last decade, many LGBT adults found
their community in the LGBT bar scene. Given the presence of
alcohol and the fact that bars are adult environments, these are
not appropriate settings for youth to meet others in their
"tribe." However, LGBTQ youth—like other youth—will sometimes find their way into bars. Thus, for many LGBTQ youth,
these settings are the first introduction to the wider LGBT
world. LGBTQ youth—again, like other youth—need to be
able to socialize and meet peers in safe, healthy, nonerotic,
alcohol-free settings.

What types of youth services do LGBTQ youth need? Basically the same types of youth services that all youth need:

- Community-based youth centers that affirm all youth
- Drop-in centers where youth can hang out
- Youth discussion groups—or more creative alternatives, like rap or poetry groups
- Afterschool programs for tutoring and studying
- Recreational programs
- School-based extracurricular sports, music, and art activities
- Service-oriented programs and volunteer opportunities
- Educational or instructional groups
- Life skills groups
- Counseling services

Generic Services Versus Special Services

There has been some debate about the need to mainstream LGBTQ young people into existing youth services programs as opposed to developing an array of specialized youth services for them. Opponents of special services note that LGBTQ young people need to interact within the larger heterosexual context of society, and claim that such programming promotes segregation rather than integration and "ghettoizes" LGBTQ youth. Those who favor programs geared specifically for LGBTQ youth claim that LGBTQ youth will not use generic services because they perceive these services as anti-LGBT. They also assert that special services could hire openly LGBT staff that could empathize with the struggles of LGBTQ youth and act as role models for their clients. Proponents of special-ized services note that youth services practitioners are often uncomfortable, unskilled, and untrained in working with LGBTQ youth, and moreover, most youth services settings are generally unsafe places for a self-identified or even a perceived LGBTQ young person.

The answer lies in a combination of both types of youth services. Services designed especially with an understanding of LGBTQ youth development (see Mallon, 1998a) could provide counseling with sensitivity to the issues important to LGBTQ youth, in an atmosphere where they feel safe (see Mallon, 1994). Ideally, special services could funnel LGBTQ youth to general, affirming agencies when required. For example, LGBTQ youth requiring life skills training could participate in these types of programs with nongay youth. At the same time, however, generic services need to be able to respond to and create LGBTQ-affirming environments for these young people. In the final analysis, specialized services for LGBTQ youth would not be necessary if mainstreamed youth services agencies were held accountable for providing quality care to all children, including LGBTQ children.

Although it is preferable for all youth to be integrated into appropriate services, until youth services practitioners and their agencies become more knowledgeable and skilled in working with homosexually oriented adolescents via training and technical assistance, it is recommended that specialized youth services programs be developed and funded to provide an array of options and serve as safe places for this underserved population of young people. Special environments for LGBTQ youth should be created when existing environments do not provide for their safety and well-being. In some settings, LGBTQ youth are given clear messages that they are not welcome.

Roberto, a 16-year-old Latino from Los Angeles, recounted this story:

> When I went to my local community center all they did was play basketball and I'm sorry, but I hate basketball. I tried to get involved with some of the youth activities, but I just didn't feel comfortable with all of those guys. I always felt like they were looking at me and judging me. I heard about this youth group at the Lesbian and Gay Center in LA and it was very scary to go there by myself, but one night I went to a meeting. As soon as I walked in I thought—"Oh, thank God, there are other kids like me!" Finally I could have some friends. Finding the youth group was the best thing that ever happened to me. I have friends, we hang out,

sometimes we go to the center, sometimes we just do what other kids do—go to the mall, go to the movies, you know, just teenager stuff.

Although it should be a goal for all youth service systems to provide affirming, safe environments for all youth, providers must also understand that LGBTQ specific youth services make LGBTQ youth no longer feel like outsiders. They are places for them to be themselves. The stress of managing one's identity can be very tiring for a young person. Being able to let loose is very important for youth. In such environments, youth can be themselves, which includes being physically affection-ate in a way that non-LGBTQ youth take for granted. Because LGBTQ youth experience stigmatization, they are sometimes either unwelcome in existing youth services environments, or feel that they are unwelcome because they do not find a niche in such a surrounding.

What Can Youth Workers Do?

How can youth services agencies create environments that sug-gest safety and acceptance? On the basis of my own experi-ences in the field, I have developed 10 recommendations for developing a safe agency environment that affirms the identity of every young person:

1. Acknowledge that LGBTQ youth are among your clients. Do not assume that all your clients are heterosexual. Many times we make assumptions based on inaccurate informa-tion or misperceptions. Just as clients will tell you who they are when—and if—they feel ready, LGBTQ clients will come out if and when they feel that there is a safe environ-ment in which they can disclose this information. Even if you do not think that you have LGBTQ youth in your organ-ization, you probably do.

2. Educate yourself and your coworkers about LGBTQ youth. Familiarize yourself with the literature, bring in speakers, or ask an openly LGBT professional to act as your "cultural

guide" to teach you and others in your agency about
LGBTQ issues.

3. Use gender-neutral language. If a practitioner uses language that assumes a person is heterosexual (i.e., inquiring
about a woman's boyfriend or husband), LGBTQ clients
may not feel that the professional is knowledgeable about
their orientation and may not share valuable information.
The use of words and terms such as "partner" or "someone
special in your life" are appropriate and it is important to
use them.

4. Use the words gay, lesbian, bisexual, transgender, and
questioning in an appropriate context when talking with
clients about diversity. As youth workers we try to be inclusive by specifically referring to the diverse groups of people
that we encounter—a Latina foster youth, a developmentally challenged boy, a low income family. Being inclusive
means also mentioning and acknowledging the existence of
LGBTQ people.

5. Have visible signs in the waiting room or in your office that
speak to the fact that it is an LGBT-affirmative environment. Magazines, pamphlets, or posters that have the words
gay, lesbian, bi, or *trans* printed on them let clients know
that your sensitized agency is a safe place for them. If you
put them up and they get torn down—and they might—put
them up again and have a discussion about why they have
such a strong impact on some people.

6. Be prepared to change the culture of your organization.
Condemning all slurs about all people lets colleagues know
that you do not think a joke is funny if it is at the expense
of any group. This sends an unambiguous message that oppression hurts everyone. Chapter 9 suggests a framework
for organizational transformation.

7. If a client discloses to you that he or she is LGBTQ, acknowledge it and talk about it. Don't just move on to other subjects.
Talk about what it means to this client to be LGBTQ. Process
the feelings with them. It's okay to let clients know that you
may not be able to answer all of their questions, or even to

acknowledge that the subject makes you feel uncomfortable because you don't have a lot of information about what it's like to be an LGBTQ person. But it is critical that you make sure that you are unconditionally accepting of the person, supportive of his or her struggle to come to terms with these complex issues, and willing to listen.

8. Do not confuse trans identity and LGB identity. Be aware that youth who identify as gender variant or trans are also members of sexual minority communities, although they may not be gay, lesbian, or bisexual. They may require services that are unique to meet their needs.

9. Research resources in the LGBT community. Identify and become familiar with the resources that exist for LGBTQ people in your geographic area. If there are services in your area, visit them. Be prepared to escort clients who might be scared to go to an LGBTQ agency for the first time.

10. If you are LGBT-identified yourself, consider coming out! Visibility is powerful. But you do not have to be an LGBT professional to work with LGBTQ youth. It is of course important to have role models that reflect back the diversity of the youth, but nongay allies are also very important.

Systemic Responses: The Need for Alternatives and Strategies

In order to create consistently safe environments, there must be system-wide policies and practices in place to support the individual responses described above.

First, providing information alone is not sufficient. There must be a system-wide recognition of the fact that negative attitudes toward homosexuality and discrimination against LGBTQ youth contribute significantly to the difficulties that these youth encounter. Youth care professionals need to acknowledge the existence of young LGBT people and develop ways to educate themselves—as well as the families of children in care—in order to understand the significance of sexual orientation in young peoples' lives.

Supporting LGBTQ youth and their families requires service providers trained in family systems and competent to address gender/sexual orientation issues in a sensitive way with children and families. Part of the youth service provider's role is to work toward increasing the parents' knowledge about LGBTQ adolescents, and to model and encourage nonjudgmental and accepting attitudes and behavior toward the youth (see PFLAG, 1990).

Providing youth services for LGBTQ youth can cause problematic public relations concerns, particularly if the system does not have a clearly defined policy to provide appropriate services for LGBTQ youth. Youth services administrators would be wise to think about how their programs can develop or adapt existing services to ensure the safety of all program participants.

Another strategy for creating a safe environment can be found in transforming the youth services system into one which is proactively responsive to the needs of LGBTQ youth. Hiring openly LGBT staff in community-based and residential programs is one step in this process. LGBTQ youth interviewed in several studies identified openly LGBTQ staff as instrumental in making them aware that the environment was safe. Closeted staff sent a clear message: "It's not safe for me to be out here— so it's not safe for you to be out, either." Jane from Toronto made this comment:

> When I walked into the center I saw this woman who worked there who I recognized from a dance I went to in the lesbian community. She looked really panicked when she saw me and then very much avoided me. In fact she went out of her way to stay away from me while I was there. When I was leaving the center she was also walking out and said to me, "Please don't tell anyone, okay? I can't be out on my job." I couldn't believe it. I never went back there again. I mean if the staff can't be open, then I knew I certainly couldn't.

Systematic and ongoing staff training and professional development for all levels of youth services personnel are also essential. Andres, an 18-year-old African American gay youth from Chicago, made this comment about staff training:

> I don't know what they teach these staff in social work school or wherever they go, but they sure don't know anything about gay and lesbian people. I think they should all be required before graduating to take a Homosexuality 101 course—you know, a class to give them the language and to tell them about us. I am sometimes so shocked by how little staff really knows about us, many of them still believe all of those old-time myths and stereotypes. It's amazing to me.

Existing youth services programs need to be particularly aware of the following underserved groups, as there are currently very few programs that focus on meeting their needs: adolescent lesbians, transgender youth, gay and lesbian youth between the ages of 12 and 15, and seriously emotionally impaired LGBT youths between the ages of 12 and 20. I am not suggesting that specialized programs be developed by youth-serving agencies serving agencies to meet these needs, but rather that these youth are vulnerable populations within an already at-risk population group, and they may require additional attention from youth workers.

6

Relationships and Dating

L GBTQ youth, like their heterosexual counterparts, enjoy
developing relationships with peers—which includes dating
and the development of romantic attachments. It is as natural
for LGBTQ youth to date and to develop romantic attachments
as it is for heterosexual youth to do this. In fact, if LGBTQ
youth are permitted to foster age and developmentally appropriate relationships during adolescence, then it is less likely
that they will have a biphasic adolescence later in their lives
and it is more likely that they will develop fully as adults who
envision having a healthy relationship in their lives.

LGBTQ youth, like all youth, want to be able to be involved
in relationships. Like all youth, LGBTQ youth have crushes,
think a lot about boys or girls that they like, and spend a great
deal of time looking at them to see how they compare with others. Dating is a natural part of any adolescence. Not being
able to date someone you like because of the stigma that is associated with an LGBTQ identity can be very difficult for sexual minority youth.

Although online relationships are a poor substitute for actual face-to-face relationships, the internet has made it possible
for LGBTQ youth who have access to computers to socialize
and meet other LGBTQ youth online. This phenomenon has

provided unprecedented opportunities for social interaction
with others in the LGBTQ community. Meeting other LGBTQ
people can, depending on geography and the need to hide, be a
difficult prospect for some LGBTQ youth. In large urban areas,
LGBTQ youth groups and gay/straight alliances in schools
make it possible for youth to get together, but in some localities
these opportunities do not exist.

LGBTQ youth frequently date people of both genders, at
least initially. Paul, a young man in Philadelphia, made this
comment:

> First I dated girls because that was what I thought I was
> supposed to do. I had a lot of friends that were girls any-
> way, so I went out with a few on dates—but there wasn't
> anything there. They were nice and all that, but there was
> no chemistry. Then, after a while, when I got the courage,
> I went out with a few guys and it was much better. There
> was something special there. But then I would date girls
> again; just to be sure that it was better with guys. It was
> kind of back and forth for a while. The whole dating thing
> was kind of like trying on a glove on your left hand that is
> really meant for your right hand—it fits, but it doesn't feel
> right—but when you switch it to the correct hand, you re-
> alize what a good fit really feels like.

Youth who have opportunities to date people that they are
attracted to emerge as healthier adolescents. But LGBT dating
may make some youth workers uncomfortable. Why? There are
several reasons:

- Society has been generally so rejecting of LGBTQ people
  that seeing them in relationships can be intimidating.
  Youth workers may have internalized the negative images of
  LGBTQ people to such an extent that they think dating behavior is wrong.
- LGBTQ youth who hug, hold hands, or kiss in public are
  often said to be "flaunting" their identity, when in reality,
  they are doing the same thing that all teenagers do.

- Youth workers might be nervous about a negative reaction from the community if they are out in the community on a trip with LGBTQ youth and the youth are acting as if they are in a relationship.

What Can Youth Workers Do?

One thing that all youth workers must ask themselves is: How comfortable am I about dealing with discussions of gender, sexuality, and sexual behavior with any youth with whom I work?

Sexuality is a huge part of adolescence. Becoming a sexual being is a major developmental task for all youth. Youth workers have varying degree of comfort or discomfort with the topic.

The first step in beginning to examine your feelings about this topic is to be self-reflective on your own values, attitudes, and feelings about all forms of sexuality. In some cases this might mean that youth workers should receive specialized training in human sexuality for adolescents. Dr. Michael Carrera, author of several wonderful books about human sexuality (1984, 1992), provides a wonderful framework for setting in motion these discussions.

Youth workers should, as part of this training, also be prepared to have open and accepting conversations with LGBTQ youth about sex, love, marriage, rearing children, having commitment ceremonies, and dating. In essence, LGBTQ youth desire the same things that all youth hope for. Youth workers should also try not to overreact to the fact that the discussions with LGBTQ youth will focus on same-gendered, rather than opposite-gendered, expressions.

Avoiding Double Standards

If your organization has policies about youth who participate in your program and who are dating, it would be a good idea to make sure that these policies are gender neutral and that all young people are aware of them. It is also a good idea to either ignore them or enforce them evenly for both opposite-gender relationships and same-gender relationships.

In many cases, what is inappropriate behavior for opposite-gender couples is also inappropriate behavior for same-gender couples. Step back from the situation at hand and ask yourself: If a boy and a girl were doing that, would I intervene, would I stop them? If your answer is yes, then it is probably appropriate to hold the same standard for a same-gender couple. If your answer is no, then deal with your own feelings and leave the youth to theirs.

> Two youth counselors in a community-based group home were summoned by the other residents to come outside to the front of the group home to see what was going on. When they arrived they witnessed two of the male residents engaging in simulated sex acts on the group home's front lawn. Shocked at first by what they saw, the workers made a quick assessment of the situation and told the boys involved to come inside. They asked the other residents to go back to what they were doing. Although distressed by what the boys were doing on the group home's front lawn, they stepped back from the situation, de-homosexualized the behavior and realized that if a boy and a girl were engaging in this type of behavior, they would know how to address it.
>
> They met with both of the boys, individually and then together, to discus why they were simulating sex. After a discussion with the boys about adolescent sexual feelings and expressions of those feelings, the boys said they were bored and that they were just "playing around." The boys said they were not involved with one another sexually and they reiterated that they were aware of the house policy that prohibited sexual relationships between residents. The staff asked them not to please not "play" like that in public places—particularly in the front of the group homes, as they were conscious about being good neighbors. At the house community meeting later that evening the issue was discussed, not as a means of belittling the youth involved, but as a way to discuss the importance of appropriate behavior in the community.

In this situation, a potentially negative situation was turned into a teaching moment by staff who kept their cool and did not allow their own discomfort with the matter at hand to cloud their thinking.

LGBTQ youth have a right to have relationships and, in fact, same-gender dating for LGBTQ youth is a healthy and natural part of their development. Despite the reality that it might make some youth workers uncomfortable, it should be nurtured and accepted as a part of all youth's development.

7

School Issues

School and school-related activities comprise a major portion of an adolescent's life. LGBTQ students must cope with unique stresses that their non-LGBTQ counterparts do not have to face. These stresses, which are related in large part to their identities as LGBTQ individuals, may interfere with school socialization, school success, and the educational process itself. LGBTQ young people are often subject to verbal taunts and harassment directly linked to their gender/sexual orientation status. At times, the harassment escalates to physical violence, which can cause LGBTQ students to be truant from school or drop out all together. The case example below illustrates the difficulties that some LGBTQ youth face in school settings:

> School was a living hell for me. It was "f****t" this and "f****t" that—all the time. It wore me out. I got so exhausted from trying to watch my back and deal with all the verbal insults that were hurled at me. I finally couldn't take it anymore and I just never went back. I took the GED and passed, that was the end of my high school career. It wasn't that I didn't like school—I just couldn't take the abuse anymore.

Schools can be very dangerous places for LGBTQ youth or even for those perceived to be.

> John lived at home with his parents and two brothers. He had a good relationship with both of his parents and his brothers. John had always been teased by peers for being gay, because he exhibited some mannerisms that have been linked to stereotypical gay features—but John identified as heterosexual. One day while in the bathroom at school, John, who had become accustomed to verbal taunts, was physically assaulted by a group of boys who called him "f****t" and "c***sucker." His injuries required that he be treated at the emergency room. John was so shaken by this experience that he requested a transfer to another school.

Although an honest and open discussion of LGBT identity is sure to evoke a great deal of discussion in school settings, it is important to remember that it is usually in school settings where children first learn that one of the worst things you can call a peer is *faggot*. This unfortunate socialization process occurs as young as in kindergarten, and becomes an everyday word that often goes unchallenged by school authorities.

Because schools are the places where most youth spend the majority of their time, schools are places that can greatly influence the thinking of all youth. Bullying and name-calling, common at schools, is hurtful behavior that affects all youth (see Mental Health America, n.d.). Although the old adage goes "sticks and stones will break my bones, but names will never hurt me," name-calling is in fact harmful and hurtful to LGBTQ youth, to those perceived to be, and in fact to all youth.

Recommendations for Schools

School-related personnel have an opportunity to stop verbal harassment, which frequently leads to physical violence. As school administrators and school boards are becoming liable

for these issues when they fail to protect students from them
more and more—e.g., after the 1996 Jamie Nabozny case in
Wisconsin, when he was awarded $900,000 in punitive dam-
ages because his school did not protect him from injury—
school settings are beginning to address ways that they can intervene. For resource materials supporting this kind of change,
see Eudey (n.d.).

Although there are several schools in the United States
specifically designed for LGBTQ youth, and some youth may
be best served by attending them, the solution is not to place
all LGBTQ youth in specialized schools, but to hold all schools
accountable for providing safe educational environments where
all youth can grow and thrive. An excellent state example of
this can be found in California. The California Safe Schools
Coalition is a statewide partnership of organizations and individuals dedicated to eliminating discrimination and harassment
on the basis of actual or perceived sexual orientation and gender identity in California schools. The primary goal of the
coalition is to ensure the effective and comprehensive imple-
mentation of the California Student Safety and Violence
Prevention Act of 2000. The act prohibits discrimination and
harassment on the basis of sexual orientation or gender identity
in California public schools. The law, authored as A.B. 537 by
then-Assembly member Sheila Kuehl and signed into law by
Governor Gray Davis, amended the state Education Code by
adding actual or perceived sexual orientation and gender identity to existing sections on discrimination. Visit www.casafe
schools.org for more.

An earlier report, *Making Schools Safe for Gay and Lesbian Youth*, published by the Massachusetts Commission of
Gay and Lesbian Youth in School in 1993, set the ground-
work for a discussion about problems faced by LGBTQ youth
in schools. The report offers a series of recommendations that
guarantee safety and end abuse. Other schools interested in
providing more gay-affirming approaches to educating
LGBTQ youth can replicate these recommendations. A complete copy of this report can be obtained online at

www.doe.mass.edu/cnp/GSA/safegl.html. Below is a review of five recommendations made in this report, which can be used as a basis for creating an LGBTQ-affirming environment in school systems.

Recommendation 1: School policies that protect LGBT students

Professionals operating in the absence of clearly stated policies utilize their own personal experiences as a guide, which in the case of dealing with LGBT-oriented youth can lead to conclusions based on cultural, religious, and societal biases. Written, formal policies help prevent discrimination, harassment, and verbal abuse of LGBTQ young people and those perceived to be. Accordingly, schools should establish policies that ensure equal access to all courses and activities for all students. Adopting and publicizing policies that ban anti-LGBTQ language and harassment on the part of the faculty and students is a simple straightforward solution that sends a clear message to the school community and costs nothing to implement. Obviously, violence of any type should not be tolerated and clear procedures should be established to deal with violent incidents.

Recommendation 2: Training for teachers and all staff

An essential component in creating safer environments for LGBTQ students is to ensure that all school staff—teachers, administrators, cafeteria staff, maintenance staff, and support staff—be equipped with accurate and relevant knowledge necessary for addressing the needs of LGBTQ young people in a caring and sensitive manner. In addition to providing violence prevention and crisis intervention training for school personnel, educational systems must also become expert in marshaling community resources to meet the needs of LGBTQ students and their families. Moreover, continued and ongoing education and training for all levels of education professionals is essential and necessary to raise the consciousness about the need to develop appropriate and safe environments for LGBTQ youth.

If educators are truly committed to diversity, then they must be willing to address the issues of sexual diversity as well. The myths of child molestation and "recruitment" of young people must also be directly confronted in order to overcome obstacles to providing competent services to LGBTQ youth and their families. Clinical theories which view LGBT identity in developmentally pejorative terms and moralistic arguments must also emerge, so that they can be defused and answered. Changes in teacher certification requirements and school accreditation requirements should also be considered.

Recommendation 3: School-based support groups for LGBTQ and non-LGBTQ students

Young people respond best to other young people. One means to this end is the development of regular support groups for LGBTQ adolescents and other students who want to talk about LGBTQ issues. Heterosexual young people also need opportunities to talk openly with their peers who are LGBT-identified. Gay/straight alliances are effective in-school support groups. Schools need to commit resources to this effort by advertising the existence of these groups and by appointing a faculty advisor to facilitate this process with the students. As guidance counselors, nurses, and school social workers are frequently among the first to address issues of sexual orientation in school systems, these professionals should receive special training to provide support and information for LGBTQ youth and their families.

Recommendation 4: Information in school libraries for LGBTQ adolescents

Young people who are or who think they might be LGBT frequently do not have access to accurate information about their own identities. Young people with questions need to have access to resources and information about LGBT issues that are readily available in school libraries. Such information should include videos, books—especially those written by young people for young people—pamphlets, and other materials for use by students, teachers, and parents. Information specifically written for the parents of LGBTQ youth is also important. Libraries should develop a reading list of books on LGBT issues and should periodically display these books and materials in a highly visible way. A well-researched local guide to LGBTQ youth organizations and organizations that support family members should also be available.

Recommendation 5: Curriculum that includes content about LGBT people

Since the classroom is the heart of the learning experience for students in educational systems, discussion about LGBTQ issues and a recognition of the contribution of LGBT people to history, literature, arts, science, and modern society should be integrated into all subject areas and departments in an age-appropriate fashion. To do this, educational systems must commit resources to examining current curriculum for bias, provide faculty development to assist teachers in developing competence in this area, and encourage and support teachers in attending conferences that focus on LGBTQ issues relevant to their subject area.

What Can Youth Workers Do?

The following are recommendations for promoting competence with respect to working with LGBTQ students and their families:

- Break the silence that surrounds issues of gender/sexual orientation and affirm all forms of diversity.
- Work toward making the environment a safe one for LGBTQ youth. Schools need to foster an environment where name-calling and slurs of all types are unacceptable. Schools must have a zero tolerance policy for physical violence of all types. Administrators should address physical violence swiftly, placing the blame clearly on those perpetrating the violence, not on the LGBTQ youth for being out about their identity.
- Schools must establish environments where it is safe for LGBT adults to be as open about their orientation as it is

for nongay staff. Role modeling by LGBT adults will benefit all students, not just LGBTQ students.

- Schools must involve parents as much as possible in discussions about gender, sexuality, and sexual identity issues. Parental education is a key factor in abolishing myths and stereotypes, as well as an effective means toward reducing the stigma associated with being LGBTQ.
- Schools should support gay/lesbian/bi/trans/straight alliances such as the Gay, Lesbian, and Straight Education Network programs or Project 10 programs, which can be found across the country.

The stressful experiences encountered by many LGBTQ youth in educational settings are cumulative and detrimental to educational performance, but also to self-esteem and sense of self-worth. Teachers, coaches, teachers' aides, social workers, guidance counselors, and administrators play key roles in both mitigating or enhancing the negative effects of the stressors associated with school life for many LGBTQ youth. School boards must also set standards for addressing these issues.

8

Health & Mental Health Issues for LGBTQ Youth

L GBTQ youth may have health and mental health needs that are unique to their status as members of a sexual minority.

Health Care Issues

According to research, LGBTQ youth have health-related issues in several key areas: reproductive health and parenting, trauma and sexual assault, eating disorders, substance abuse, suicidal ideation, and sexually transmitted diseases (STDs). Access to preventive and restorative health care services may also pose special difficulties for sexual minority youth. There are significant social barriers to self-disclosure of gender/sexual orientation and sexual behavior, and the reluctance of youth to disclose may impede the diagnosis and treatment of medical conditions. Additional barriers include costs, lack of available and adolescent-specific health services, lack of transportation, and inability of some LGBTQ youth to follow up with appointments (see Ryan & Futterman, 1998). The harsh reality and environmental consequences of living life on the streets compound the risks for LGBTQ runaway and homeless youth.

What are the specific health care problems that exist for LGBT youth? The limited literature that is available suggests that the profiles for each subgroup—gay, lesbian, bisexual, and transgender—differ significantly.

Young lesbians frequently note the discomfort that they experience in seeking gynecological care, as suggested by this young woman's comments:

> Every time I went to the gynecologist, he always asked me if I was sexually active, and when I responded that I was, then he immediately asked what form of contraceptives I used. When told him "none," I got this big lecture about unplanned pregnancy, and not getting pregnant. I never felt comfortable telling him that the form of sexuality that I was engaged in, namely with another female, could not get me pregnant. I just didn't think he could handle it. I did have a lot of health care concerns, but usually I got so turned off by his assumption that I was straight that I just clammed right up and stayed quiet.

Although not all LGBTQ youth are sexually active, some are. Additionally, research shows that most young lesbians have been sexually active with males. Just like straight young women, lesbians who engage in sexual relationships with men sometimes become pregnant. These young women need guidance and advice on reproductive health and parenting. Many youth providers who work with pregnant teens make the assumption that because they are pregnant they must be heterosexual. This is a practice error. The same is true for gay young men who father children—not all of these young people are heterosexual just because they have engaged in heterosexual sexual contact.

Gay males concerned with body image may also be at risk for eating disorders. This does not seem to be a common issue for young lesbians, although the majority of eating disorders in adolescents are found in the heterosexual female population.

Substance abuse is a leading health concern for LGBTQ youth. The numbing effects of alcohol and other substances can be an effective means of anesthetizing oneself from isolation and vulnerability. LGBTQ youth abuse substances for the same reasons as their heterosexual counterparts: to self-medicate, to relieve tension, to increase feelings of self-esteem, to experiment, and to assert independence. In some cases, LGBTQ youth may also abuse substances to manage stigma and shame, to deny same-gender feelings, and in some cases to fit in with a peer group.

Lesbians, bisexual youth, questioning youth, gay males, and transgender youth are at high risk for violence, which was addressed directly in Chapter 4. Frequently, this population includes many victims of assault, including rape and sexual assault. More than half of all rape victims are adolescents. Most reported cases are women, but males are also victimized. Due to the fact that transgender youth challenge societal norms around gender, they are at particularly high risk for sexual assault and violence. Transgender youth have other health-related concerns that are unique to their status. These are addressed directly in Chapter 10.

Mental Health Issues

Although homosexuality was deleted from the American Psychiatric Association's *Diagnostic and Statistical Assessment Manual* in 1973, some mental health professionals still act as though a gay, lesbian, or transgender identity is curable. Indeed, there are some clinicians who claim to be able to "cure" homosexuality through reparative or aversion therapies. Research has shown that these efforts have been unsuccessful, and while one's sexual behavior is changed, one's sense of internal goodness of fit remains lesbian, gay, bisexual, or transgender. Contemporary clinical approaches to working with LGBTQ youth do not attempt to change the young person's sexual orientation, but work with youth from an LGBTQ-affirming perspective.

Youth providers must understand that it is not because one is LGBTQ that mental health services are required. Rather, the stress inherent in living life as a stigmatized person leads many LGBTQ people to seek mental health services. LGBTQ youth who seek care may actually be more resilient and may have more effective coping skills than those who do not seek assistance. It is also important to note that youth may need mental health services as a result of childhood trauma and stresses, or another organic impairment not directly related to their sexual orientation.

Although some young people genuinely can be diagnosed with gender identity disorder—namely, transgender youth— most gay, lesbian, and bisexual youth are comfortable with their gender as male or female, but identify clearly as gay, lesbian, or bisexual. Many inadequately trained mental health professionals erroneously use the diagnostic category of gender identity disorder for a gay, lesbian, or bisexual youth. For more discussion, see Chapter 10.

LGBTQ youth seem to most often be seen by mental health practitioners for depression, anxiety, suicidal behavior, somatic disorders, chronic stress, and gender identity issues.

Chronic stress from verbal harassment is a common theme identified by researchers investigating the experiences of LGBTQ youth. Coming out to family, fearing being found out, negotiating safety, and managing one's LGBTQ identity are additional stressors that these youth face. These factors can contribute to eroding an LGBTQ youth's sense of self-worth, self-esteem, and confidence, and can lead to youth needing treatment. In addition, the need to hide distorts almost everything about a young LGBTQ person's life, but this also promotes dysfunction and can cause a youth to seek help. The most frequently abused youth are transgender youth who do not or cannot meet traditional culturally defined versions of masculinity or femininity.

Depression

Depression is characterized by deep persistent sadness, lack of pleasure, and in some cases helplessness and hopelessness. Because most LGBTQ youth may initially feel isolated and unsure of their orientation, unable to identify others like them, and because of this may believe that there is something wrong with them, depression is fairly common. Depression also occurs with other symptoms such as anxiety, eating disorders, substance abuse, and chronic illness. Many youth who make suicide attempts are depressed, and depression and substance abuse are closely correlated with suicide attempts.

Suicide

Suicide is one of the highest risk behaviors among youth today. Almost one out of every five youth reports considering suicide within the past year, and 13% actually planned it. Suicide is now the third leading cause of death among teens ages 15-24, with 86% of deaths from males and 14% from females (Guzman & Bosch, 2007). There is substantial evidence to suggest that LGBTQ youth are at greater risk for suicidality (Remafedi, Farrow, & Deisher, 1991; Remafedi, French, Story, Resnick, & Blum, 1998). With these facts in mind, youth workers should be prepared to assess an individual's risk for making a suicide attempt. Youth workers should be aware of the risk factors for suicide. These include:

- A history of previous suicide attempts
- A history of substance abuse
- A history of psychiatric diagnosis, especially depression and bipolar disorder; anxiety, conduct, and personality disorders can also be indicators
- A family history of suicide
- The suicide of a peer or a friend
- Life events that involve shame or humiliation; arrests, assaults, or disciplinary incidents at school are typical events that trigger suicide attempts in vulnerable youth.

Youth workers making an assessment of a youth's suicidal ideation should consider asking the following questions as a part of their assessment:

- Have you ever felt so sad that you considered hurting yourself?
- Have you ever thought about suicide?
- How often—and how many times a day—do you think of suicide?

- Have you ever thought about how you might hurt or try to kill yourself?
- Do you have a plan for how you might kill yourself? What is it?
- Are you considering doing this now?

Youth who are deemed to be at risk for suicide will at the very least need supportive youth workers to talk with. Staff will need to share this information with a supervisor, and will be responsible for seeking appropriate referrals for the youth at community-based health clinics (see Remafedi et al., 1991, 1998). In some cases, when it is deemed that the risk is high, the youth might require in-patient hospitalization to ensure a safe environment.

Psychiatric Hospitalizations

Like heterosexual youth who suffer from severe psychiatric disorders, some LGBTQ youth may require psychiatric hospitalization. Historically, mental health in-patient settings have ignored sexual identity issues, or have made them the inappropriate focus of treatment. It is not uncommon to find mental health professionals who still view homosexuality as a psychopathology.

While there are many issues that present a challenge to adolescent treatment facilities, including the availability of adolescent-friendly mental health services, having a self-identified LGBTQ youth may cause quite a commotion for staff. When in-patient treatment is warranted, youth providers should assess the facility's ability to appropriately treat an LGBTQ youth. This assessment should include a review of their attitudes, therapeutic approaches, and past experiences in working with LGBTQ youth.

The National Center for Lesbian Rights in San Francisco has for many years coordinated a legal advocacy program for LGBTQ youth who have been institutionalized and subjected to involuntary aversion therapy for sexual orientation. Transgender youth, as the next vignette suggests, may be at particular risk for hospitalization for gender-nonconforming behavior:

Janet, an 18-year-old self-identified transgender male-to-female youth, was hospitalized in a residential treatment center in Utah. Confronted by mental health professionals and family who asked "Why can't you be more like a boy?", Janet struggled to defend her identity as a female. Despite all clinical efforts, she was steadfast in maintaining her identity. After six months of treatment, all of which was unsuccessful at converting Janet from a female to a male, Janet was discharged on her 18th birthday.

Daphne Scholinski's memoir *The Last Time I Wore a Dress* (1997) provides a real-life illustration of the experience of forced hospitalization for gender nonconformity.

What Can Youth-Serving Agencies Do?

Agencies that provide mental health services can use the form on the next page as a sample of an assessment for sensitivity.

Organizational Assessment for Competent Practice with LGBTQ Youth

	Yes	No
Has the organization worked with LGBTQ clients in the past?	❏	❏
How often are LGBTQ youth seen at the organization?	❏	❏
Are providers familiar with the needs of LGBTQ youth?	❏	❏
Do agency policies include LGBTQ youth?	❏	❏
Do agency brochures and outreach materials include LGBTQ youth?	❏	❏
Are any openly LGBT staff employed by the organization?	❏	❏
Does the organization have linkages with other LGBTQ youth organizations?	❏	❏

Describe the organization's treatment philosophy for working with LGBTQ youth. _____

_____

_____

_____

How often and what type of training has the organization's staff had in working with LGBTQ youth?_____

_____

_____

_____

9

Out-of-Home Programs for LGBTQ Youth

Most LGBTQ young people are not placed in residential settings. In fact, the majority of LGBTQ youth live with their families and never rely on a foster home, a group home, or a shelter at all. Those adolescents who do come to the attention of an out-of-home placement are young people who have experienced difficulties within their family system to such a degree that they cannot or should not continue to live at home (see DeSetta, 2003, for some compelling stories written by youth who have lived the experience). These LGBTQ youth live in residential programs, foster homes, and juvenile justice centers (Wilber, Ryan, & Marksamer, 2006).

Although some LGBTQ youth are thrown out of their homes when they disclose their gender/sexual identity or when they are found out by their families, not all of them enter out-of-home care systems because of issues directly related to their gender/sexual orientation. Like their heterosexual counterparts, the majority of LGBTQ young people were placed there before or during the onset of adolescence. Many were placed for the same reasons that other young people are: family disintegration; divorce, death, or illness of a parent; parental substance abuse or alcoholism; or physical abuse and neglect.

Living apart from one's family is seldom easy. Out-of-home systems have long been and continue to be an integral part of youth services (see Bullard, Owens, Richmond, & Alwon, 2010). The structure of the different types of residential programs varies widely and can take many forms. They range from small community-based group homes and short-term respite care or shelter facilities to large congregate care institutions that provide long-term or custodial care. Some facilities have a juvenile justice component to them, some are foster care programs, and others still are programs designed for runaway and homeless youth. All of these different types of services share one common feature, however: they provide care for children and youth on a 24-hour-a-day basis, which is very different from other youth services that are not residential in nature.

Generally, most group homes, juvenile facilities, and shelters are staffed by individual youth care workers or counselors who are employed by an agency to work in shifts to cover the facility 24 hours a day. The youth care workers who work in group home settings play a very important role in the lives of the young people in their care. Nevertheless, they are generally the lowest paid—and in many cases have obtained the least education and training—in the youth services system. The daily stress of working with adolescents in these settings, combined with the poor pay, can make it difficult for staff to be empathetic and compassionate in their dealings with the young people, and these factors also account for a high staff turnover.

Most out-of-home care settings for adolescents focus on preparing these young people for the transition to adulthood—on or before their 18th birthday, or 21st birthday in some states. Some group homes are warm, loving, and accepting of diversity and some are cold, poorly maintained, and rigid. LGBTQ young people live in and speak about both.

LGBTQ Youth in Out-of-Home Settings

There have always been LGBTQ young people in North America's out-of-home care settings but it has often been difficult for professionals to recognize their existence for three reasons: (1) many of these youth do not fit the gender-nonconforming stereotypes that most practitioners associate with an LGBTQ orientation, (2) LGBTQ young people are socialized to hide, and (3) some residential youth services professionals are contemptuous of a homosexual orientation. In addition, most professionals are completely lacking in knowledge about normal LGBTQ adolescent development. Many administrators of residential youth service agencies are fearful that acknowledging a self-identified LGBT young person in their program might be seen as encouraging or promoting an LGBT identity.

The end result is that LGBTQ youth often remain hidden and invisible in residential systems, and if they do come out, they are not provided with the same quality of care that is extended to their heterosexual counterparts.

The reflections of one gay young man about his placement experience in New York are representative of the views of many and provide a framework for examining the salient features of this issue. José, a 17-year-old Latino gay male, had several placements in and around New York City.

> I wasn't even sure that I was gay, but I knew that I liked guys. One day when I was talking on the phone to this guy that I liked, my mother overheard our conversation and figured out what was going on. She started screaming at me, telling me I was sick, that I was crazy, and saying that I needed some kind of help.
>
> I was so upset, because she really caught me off guard. I wasn't ready to tell her anything about myself—she just found me out. After an hour of screaming she kinda calmed down and told me it was just a phase that I was going through. Things were tense during that week, she didn't tell my stepfather, she was afraid of what might happen if she told him. He often lost his temper and sometimes when he was angry he would hit me. Toward the end of the week my mother told me that she was going to send me to the Dominican Republic for the summer—

there she said, "They will cure you." I had no choice, I had to go.

In September, I returned—obviously I hadn't changed, but I lied and told her that I did. She realized after two weeks that I had not changed and things just deteriorated from that point.

Finally, the silent treatment really got to me and I asked my mother to place me. I had some friends in a group home and I thought maybe that I'd be better there. Most kids don't ask their families to place them, but I did, I just couldn't take living at home anymore.

Once I was in placement, I thought it would be better, but it just got worse. I was scared to tell anyone that I was gay because I saw how the gay kids got treated—even if they thought you were gay you were treated badly. Gay kids were not treated equally; they were treated like they were not normal, like they were not human. It was hell to live there—I felt like I was trapped in some f***ing cage, I had no one to talk to, I wasn't happy.

It was like I was abnormal—like I didn't fit in the crowd. Most of the kids were pretty cruel to gay kids, but the staff . . . they were worse. One night this group of kids approached me about having sex with them, but I told them no. They were really aggressive and told me that if I didn't give it up, they'd tell the staff that I approached them. Well . . . I didn't give it up and they did just what they said they'd do—they told staff that I had made sexual advances toward them. The staff met with me, I told them what really happened, but they didn't believe me. They said "All you f****ts are just into the same thing—we've seen this before."

The next day the people from the city came and placed me in another group home. That one was worse. I got jumped by a couple of kids on the first night and the staff there wouldn't even talk to me. It was terrible there. I was treated so badly; I would just go in my room and cry. One day, after all the teasing and harassment, I just couldn't take it any more and I complained to the social worker who was kinda new herself. She said she understood and then helped get me placed in another group home, one that she said was gay friendly. This worker ended up being the only person who was cool with me. Months later I figured out that she was gay too.

This social worker always said she knew I was gay and that I should come out, but I denied that I was. She tried to reassure me that she could work with me—but I knew better. I saw how they treated the kids who were openly gay and I saw how they treated me because they thought I was gay, so there was no way that I was going to confirm it for them. I didn't want to reveal it to them because I was afraid of how they would treat me if they knew for sure. She kept pressuring me, but I refused to tell her anything. I always tried to act so straight to fit into their crowd—to fit into what they did—but I couldn't.

One day, the day when I told her I couldn't take it any more—my social worker told me that there was this place where I would feel comfortable—she said it was a place for "people like me," a place where I would fit in. But even then, I kept denying that I was gay. They scheduled a visit for me anyway. Even though they made it seem like I had a choice about whether to go there or not, I guess that they didn't really want me, I guess they wanted me out—so I was transferred to [the new residential center] and there I felt comfortable right away.

Finally I had people that I could relate to, people who I could talk to. When I first got here, I was so happy—they had this sign that said, "Here, we respect everyone! Regardless of race, religion, sexual orientation, culture, class, gender, and ability." I was so relived; I didn't have to hide nothing from anybody. I could dress the way I wanted to, I could walk the way I wanted to, I could be free, I didn't have to hide—I could be myself. It was the first time I ever felt that way.

Although treatment of LGBT youth in many out-of-home care settings is improving, stories like José's are not uncommon. LGBTQ young people in residential care report both positive and negative responses to their sexual orientation, though the negative stories outnumber the positive. Several themes emerge from the above vignette and stories like it. These themes, discussed below, are useful in understanding the experiences of LGBTQ youth in residential settings.

Invisibility and Hiding

LGBTQ young people in residential settings are frequently an invisible population. This allows administrators and staff to convince themselves that there are no LGBTQ young people in their care. Professional staff and administrators often associate LGBT identity with gender non-conformity. They believe that they would be able to identify the LGBTQ clients if there were any. Often, only those individuals who do not conform to traditional gender stereotypes (i.e., the butch girl or the effeminate boy) are identified as gay or lesbian, and are subsequently treated with disdain. The majority of LGBTQ young people are silent and hidden witnesses to the negative attitudes of staff, administrators, and peers toward those who workers believe to be LGBT-identified. Most LGBTQ young people in out-of-home settings receive—from multiple sources—the message: "Stay in the closet! We do not want to deal with this!"

Stress and Isolation

Living in the closet, as so many LGBTQ young people in foster care are forced to do, is the source of a high level of stress and isolation in their lives. The comments of Brenda, a 20-year-old lesbian from Los Angeles, exemplify this:

> I tried to hide it 'cause I saw how they treated those kids who they thought were gay or lesbian. I mean, they were treated terribly—just because the others thought they were gay. I knew that I was gay, so imagine how they would treat me if they ever found out. I felt so alone, so isolated, like

no one ever knew the real me. I couldn't talk to anybody about who I was. It was a horrible experience. Trying to hide who you really are is very difficult and exhausting. Sometimes I felt so bad I just wanted to kill myself.

Multiple Placements

Moving from one's family to a residential setting is, in and of itself, stressful. Subsequent moves from one placement to another have been identified as a major difficulty for youth in residential settings. The constant challenge of adapting to a new environment is unsettling, provokes anxiety, and undermines one's sense of permanence. Unlike other adolescents in residential settings who move from setting to setting because of individual behavioral problems, LGBTQ youth report that their sexual orientation itself led to multiple and unstable placements.

Young people report experiencing unstable placements for four reasons: they are not accepted because staff have difficulties dealing with their sexual orientation; they feel unsafe due to their sexual orientation and either AWOL (run away) from the placement for their own safety or request new placements; they are perceived as a management problem by staff because they are open about their sexual orientation; or they are not accepted by peers due to their sexual orientation.

Andrea, an 18-year-old white lesbian from New York, provides a narrative:

> I couldn't live at home with my mother, because she couldn't deal with the fact that I was a dyke. So, let me give you the sequence. I currently live at the [residence], which is a runaway and homeless youth shelter. But I was first placed in a diagnostic center. . . . But I left there after about 10 minutes when I could tell that they couldn't deal with my orientation. I AWOLed from there and stayed at my friend's house. They [the center staff] didn't say anything about me being a lesbian, but it was d**n obvious that they had a problem with me. If I felt that they couldn't deal with me, I just AWOLed—I mean my feeling was, I couldn't live

at home because my mother couldn't deal with it, and if the staff in the group home can't deal with it either, then why bother sticking around? After that I went back to my mother, then to [one group home] and then to [another group home] which is another of [an organization of] group homes, then to where I am now.

Many agencies simply get rid of LGBTQ youth because staff cannot deal with the youths' gender or sexual orientation. Many of these youth have been put in multiple placements or re-placements by agencies at all levels of care. Wilem, a 19-year-old Latino from New York, provides this account:

I have had so many [placements], I can't even remember. Too many to remember, all of those overnights . . . a lot of places. I was 14 when I went to my first one, I've been to lots of them, but I kept running away because I just couldn't live there. I even was running away from home because I didn't want anyone to know that I was gay. . . . [The worst placement] wasn't horrible but it still wasn't the best place to be. I stayed at [a group home] for a while because I met some gays there that I knew from outside, so we hung out together and they showed me the ropes.

These case examples exemplify the ways in which LGBTQ young people are continuously faced with having to negotiate new environments, many of which are inhospitable and lacking in the conditions necessary for healthy psychological development.

Replacement and Feelings of Rejection

The majority of LGBTQ young people sense that they are not welcome in most residential settings. They perceive that they are reluctantly accepted into some placements and consequently feel isolated and have negative reactions to their residential settings. Many young people are impassioned about their maltreatment in these settings, as this quotation from Wilem illustrates:

How was I treated? You mean the way we were treated? It
sucks, it sucks. I mean I wouldn't want to go back to one.
It's hard enough being in a situation when you are away
from your family and then having somebody else put you
down . . . I mean, it's just not fair.

Some young people report that they left their placement
once they realized that they were not welcomed. Maura recalls
this experience vividly:

As soon as I get discriminated against, I leave. I mean
when I was on a psychiatric ward they were trying to give
me aversion therapy, and I mean they were supposed to
help me with my depression, not by telling me that I'm
wrong. Where I am now, they are fine, but in other places
definitely there were problems. I mean when I was in [a
group home], they were giving me my own room because I
was gay to keep the other kids away from me. It's the kids
and the staff that treat you differently.

Frequently, young people who leave placements become lost
in the system, and their multiple placements create a sense of
impermanence and drift.

Verbal Harassment and Physical Violence

Many young people enter residential placements because they
offer sanctuary from abusive family relationships and violence
in their homes. However, with the constant threat of harassment and violence within the system, LGBTQ youth report being unable to feel completely secure or confident. Although violence and harassment may be an unfortunate component of
residential care from time to time for all youth, LGBTQ young
people, unlike their heterosexual counterparts, are targeted for
attack specifically because of their gender or sexual orientation. One transgender youth recalled the nightmare of verbal
harassment and physical violence:

I was coming home to the shelter one night from my job and I was just minding my own business when these three boys from the shelter started to yell at me—"Hey, you she-male, what are you anyway, a guy or a girl?" I tried to ignore them and walked a bit faster to get to the shelter, but they kept following me—taunting me, embarrassing me in front of all of these people on the street. I felt so humiliated, so bad, so low. Finally one of them jumped me from behind, pulled up my skirt, and tried to sexually assault me with his fingers. That's when someone stopped their car and yelled for them to stop. They ran, and this guy got out of his car and asked if I was all right—I said I was because I was embarrassed and humiliated—but I was hurt, inside more than outside. I didn't go back to the shelter that night or any other night. I had some money so I rented a cheap room for the night and then I went to stay with friends. It was a terrible experience, but I never reported it—I figured no one would do anything about it.

What Can Youth Workers Do?

Youth service professionals need to know how to react to these harsh realities. The most important first step is to remember that all youth service professionals have the ethical and moral responsibility to create and maintain safe environments for *every* young person in their care. The establishment of such safety is at the very core of all youth services practice.

Simple solutions cannot be found simply by trying to identify LGBTQ young people. Safe environments are essential for young people who are LGBTQ to come out, if they chose to come out. The problems encountered by LGBTQ adolescents and their families are frequently ignored and largely unrecognized by the majority of youth services professionals—analogous to the ways in which the youth services system has been deficient in addressing the specific needs of diverse ethic and racial minorities. Youth workers need to know it's crucial to develop an understanding of the impact of societal stigmatization of LGBTQ individuals and their families in order to recognize and respond to the needs of this population.

Effecting changes in attitudes and beliefs in pursuit of competent practice with LGBTQ adolescents and their families requires education, training, and self-exploration on both the individual and institutional level (see Lambda Legal Defense and Education Fund, 2001; Mallon, 2001, 2008, 2009; Wornoff & Mallon, 2006). The development of competence in this area holds promise for preserving and supporting families and for the establishment of appropriate LGBT-affirmative out-of-home services for these young people and their families.

10

Working with Transgender and Gender Variant Youth

Transgender youth are among the most misunderstood and most marginalized members of our society. With few exceptions (Mallon, 1999, 2009) there are very few research studies of transgender youth, and even fewer resource documents that social service providers can use to educate themselves about the population. These very same professionals who have the responsibility to protect and care for these young people are at times without adequate knowledge about how to work competently with them. Although trans youth have many stress-related issues and concerns, it must be emphasized that many of the psychosocial difficulties that transgender and gender variant youth experience typically are not because of gender identity, but are products of the social environment that the youth experiences—including at school and on the streets—and the lack of acceptance of the youth's gender within those environments.

Youth workers who work with trans youth need to have a basic knowledge about these young people. Entire books have been written about trans youth—in the pages that follow, the key issues of working with trans youth will be discussed, but I urge readers to see Mallon (2009) and Brill & Pepper (2008) for a full discussion of the wide range of issues pertaining to trans and gender variant youth.

Family Issues

Coming out as transgender is challenging for everyone. Some male or female teenagers who experience a trans identity may do so in secret, never telling their families and friends about it. As adults, some may continue to keep their identity private, sometimes seeking approval through transgender support groups and often in internet communities; others will be more open about their trans identity. Those who disclose their trans identity to their families may experience a variety of reactions, ranging from loving acceptance to complete rejection.

If an adolescent's trans identity is disclosed to his or her parents, it is likely to precipitate an emotional crisis for the entire family. A female-bodied trans youth's identity may be disguised as a "tomboy" phase that a daughter stubbornly refuses to grow out of, causing friction within the family only later. If a youth is intent on gender transition, however, major changes are ahead for the entire family. Being out about sexual orientation is usually a choice for some gay sons and lesbian daughters, but hiding is rarely an option for those who are entering a gender transition, because gender and gender presentation are so visible. Moreover, the changes arising from gender transition will be much more profound than just physical appearances, including emotional and hormonal changes.

While an increasing number of parents are acknowledging their child's gender struggle, most trans youth may try to keep their gender issues secret until they cannot hold them back any longer. For this cohort, their disclosure takes most parents by surprise. Moms and dads of these kids then must deal not only with shock, denial, anger, grief, misplaced guilt, and shame, but also with many real concerns about the safety, health, surgery, employment, and potential future relationships of their children. In addition, the family system must learn to call their family member by a new name—and even more difficult, begin to use new pronouns.

Mental Health and Health Concerns

When a trans youth comes out, the ability to pass in their new gender is sometimes limited—development of a sense of "realness" is a very important issue for most trans youth. Realness is not only about passing (being perceived as real), but also about feeling real inside. Hormonal therapy, a very controversial area, especially in youth-serving systems, can take years to produce a passable appearance and may have some health risks as well.

Trans youth often feel that their true gender identity is crucial to the survival of self. If their parents refuse to permit their gender transition, or if their families and friends withhold support, these youth may encounter the same risks faced by gay and lesbian youth with nonaccepting families (Burgess, 2009). Some may run away from home and live on the streets, or they may seek to escape the pain of their lives through abusing substances. Like LGB youth, trans youth also are at significantly higher risk for suicide than the average American teen.

Because of severe employment discrimination, homeless or runaway transgender youth may need to find work in the sex industry in order to survive and pay for their hormones, electrolysis, cosmetic surgery, and gender reassignment surgery. This part of the population, therefore, is at increased risk for HIV/AIDS and other sexually transmitted diseases, and should be referred to understanding, compassionate, trans-friendly health care providers for evaluation and treatment. For more on homeless or runaway LGBTQ youth, see Chapter 11.

Many transgender youth face discrimination in health care settings because they are gender variant. Fearing rejection, ridicule, and harassment, many transgender youth will not seek the services of mainstream health care systems. Youth with gender identity issues frequently experiment with hormones, often obtained illegally on the streets. The work of Annelou L.C. de Vries, Peggy T. Cohen-Kettenis, and Henriette Delemarre-Van de Waal (2006), *Clinical Management of Gender Dysphoria in*

Adolescents, is particularly useful to practitioners. Youth workers should also become familiar with the World Professional Association for Transgender Health (WPATH) *Standards of Care* (2001), formerly known as the Harry Benjamin Standards, available online at www.wpath.org.

Although not all transgender people opt for genital reassignment surgery, some do. Genital reassignment surgery during adolescence is not an option; however, medically supervised hormonal therapy and ongoing counseling are options that can and should be explored. Ingesting or injecting street hormones or high-dose hormones without medical supervision is also commonplace and may result in lethal complications. Hormonal sex reassignment can be safely done only under the supervision of an experienced endocrinologist following the WPATH standards (2001). Some trans youth who are impatient with the slow pace of hormonal sex reassignment may seek silicone injections to immediately improve their body shape and may experiment with androgen blockers or other substances, which may prove to have some health risks later in life (Wren, 2000). Often, trans youth in youth-serving systems, frustrated with that system's slowness and reluctance to arrange for hormonal treatments, buy street hormones as a group and have "pump parties," where they inject large amounts of hormones and/or whatever else is in the syringes they buy. This admittedly risky behavior is often labeled by law enforcement and child protective workers as "acting out," when it is actually adaptive behavior on the part of youth who desperately want to be, and feel, "real."

Referral for Hormonal and Surgical Sex Reassignment

Trans youth may go to extraordinary lengths to obtain relief from their gender dysphoria (see Dreifus, 2005, for a thorough discussion of this topic). The compelling need to modify the body to conform to one's gender identity cannot be adequately explained by someone who is transgender, nor can it be fully understood by someone who is not (see Israel and Tarver, 1997, for a complete discussion of this area). This self-perceived need becomes a determined drive, a desperate search for relief and release from one's own body. Trans youth face an urgent need to match their external appearance with their internal feelings, in order to achieve harmony of spirit and shape, of body and soul. The urgency itself cannot be easily understood (see Pazos, 2009, for a discussion of female-to-male transition, and Glenn, 2009, for a discussion of the male-to-female transition).

Although parents and child welfare professionals may be alarmed by a young person's desire for physical transition, it is important that they recognize the intensity fueling that desire. Referral to a psychotherapist or social worker experienced in trans issues who can conduct a proper assessment and arrive at a correct diagnosis is the key first step. Genital reassignment surgery is an extensive, complicated process, which can only be embarked upon after the individual has been evaluated and received counseling by professionals specifically trained in this area. As noted above, this is not an option for adolescents.

Gender Identity Disorder

From a strictly diagnostic perspective, if the young person meets the criteria as established for Gender Identity Disorder (GID) in DSM-IV (American Psychological Association, 1994) in childhood, it is not difficult to make a diagnosis. Based on the sketchy history of this diagnostic category, however, one must also consider whether GID is really a disorder. One of the criteria for a disorder is whether the person diagnosed is distressed by their condition. Are gender variant young people distressed by their condition, and if so, what is the source of their distress? Or do they become distressed when they are told that they cannot be what they are sure they are? Or are they distressed because of the social ostracism they must endure?

In my own clinical experiences with transgender adolescents, young people have been more harmed than helped by clinicians who insist on "correcting" the gender variant child by attempting to make him or her more gender-conforming. One needs only to read the superb memoir of Scholinski (1987), the powerful work of Feinberg (1993), or the compelling story by Colapinto (2001) to see that these attempts to "correct" for gender variance fail miserably. Professionals are directed to the work of Bartlett, Vasey, & Buowski (2000) and Langer & Martin (2004) as well for a thorough discussion of this debate. With true transgender young people, no treatment program, no residential program, no child welfare program, no group therapy, and no aversion treatment plan can change who they are.

Family Reactions to Transgender Youth

More often than not, I have seen parents who are greatly distressed by their gender variant child. Even mild, typical gender nonconformity sends terror into the hearts of most parents. One mother panicked when her 6-year-old son asked for an Easy-Bake Oven. When I asked what was so scary, she said the oven was a "girl toy," and asked for my advice. I told her that if she could afford it, she should buy it—in a few weeks, the oven would either be her child's favorite toy, or be cast aside in favor of the next new toy.

Such advice provides no solace for other parents. They are embarrassed, guilty, ashamed, and fearful that somehow their parenting is to blame for what "went wrong," as the following case illustrates:

> Jon was a 13-year-old American-born Trinidadian child referred by his great-grandmother's Medicaid social worker. Jon was of average intelligence; he was from a working class family and was living in a housing project in Manhattan. On the day of the interview, Jon arrived for the interview dressed in boy's clothing, but with a very clear girl's hairstyle. His great-grandmother, who was his primary caretaker and 85 years old, accompanied Jon. An obvious warm and affectionate relationship existed between the two, although some negative feelings also existed because of Jon's insistence that he was a girl. Jon's great-grandmother explained that it was causing her great distress that Jon was

insisting that he was a girl. She feared losing her standing in the community because neighbors began to ask her what she had done to make the child "that way." She was embarrassed by Jon's cross-dressing, by his insistence on being called by his preferred name, Simone, and by other gender nonconforming mannerisms and behaviors. Jon simply said, "I can't be what I am not, and I am not a boy." Jon's great-grandmother said to the interviewer, "Mister, I have one question for you. Can you change him back?" When the response was no, she said, "Then you can keep him."

As she got up to leave, the interviewer stopped her and explained that she could not leave her great-grandson with him. Then they explored the possibility of family supports for her and her great-grandson and discussed the possibility of out-of-home placement options. Both of these prospects were quite dismal; transgender children and youth are not accepted easily in child welfare agencies, nor are there many competent practitioners in the field. After some discussion, the great-grandmother agreed that he could stay at home with her, but they settled on a treatment plan that included some compromises for both of them. It was not an ideal plan, but it was better than an out-of-home placement.

Although some are healthy and resilient, many gender variant children are at great risk within their family system and within institutional structures (Cooper, 2009). Gender variant children and youth, because they are told that they do not fit in, are in a constant search for an affirming environment where they can be themselves. In the search for this situation, many transgender youth are at risk for the associated symptomlogy of depression, anxiety, self-abuse, substance abuse, suicide, and family violence. In their desperate search for affirmation, they often place themselves in risky environments.

Parents seeking to find answers may seek to have their transgender child "cured" through punishment, physical violence, or endless mental health assessments. Transgender young people may be locked in their rooms, forced to wear their hair in gender-typical styles or dress in gender-typical clothing, and denied opportunities to socialize. Transgender young people, as in the filmic story of Ludovic (Berliner & Scotta, 1997), are viewed as the problem in the family. Such classification leads the family to scapegoat the child, and he or she becomes the reason for everything that goes wrong. Families may begin to project their anxieties about other family conflicts on the transgender child as a way of avoiding confronting the real issues.

Some transgender youth are shipped away to behavioral camps, psychiatric hospitals, or residential treatment facilities, where rigidly enforced gender conformity further represses their needs and does more harm than good. In 35 years of experience in child welfare, I have rarely have come across a mental health professional or social worker who is knowledgeable and proficient about working with a transgender youth in an affirming manner. Most do not understand the condition, and few have ever had training to prepare them for competent practice with transgender youth. At present, very few gender-specialized services exist in mental health and child welfare systems across the country. Regrettably, most schools of social work are not preparing practitioners to respond to the needs of this population.

Israel and Tarver (1997) observe, "As there are no treatment models for curing transgender feelings, needs and behaviors, one is left to wonder what types of treatment transgender children and youth endure at the hands of parents and professionals. Such treatment approaches are little more than abuse, professional victimization, and profiteering under the guise of support for a parent's goals" (pp. 134–135). Brill and Pepper (2008), however, offer trans-affirming perspectives of diagnosis and treatment, and provide a thorough examination of the clinical and social issues affecting trans youth. Such guidance is welcome where affirming literature on this topic is scarce.

Transgender Young People in Educational Settings

Educational settings, unfortunately, are among the least affirming environments for gender variant young people. School officials who perceive children and adolescents as gender variant target them as individuals to be closely monitored for "acting out" behaviors. In their riveting film *Out in the Cold*, Criswell and Bedogne (2002) document the extent to which gender atypical youths are rejected by families and the institutions they were raised to believe in, especially school.

Gender variant boys will likely be mercilessly teased for not being rough-and-tumble, and ill-informed adults might assume that these boys are gay. Some are moved toward what I term "the sports corrective." They are pushed into organized sports teams as if participation in such activities will "correct" their gender nonconformity. Gender variant girls are also verbally harassed for being too much like boys and not enough like girls; they are almost always confronted by both peers and adults who try to enroll them in what I call "the etiquette corrective." The idea is to turn them from tomboys into ladies. It seldom, if ever, works for them, and only adds to the pain and the self-blame, as this vignette from Scholinski (1997) illustrates:

> Pinning me to the ground, the girls at school forced red lipstick onto my mouth . . . the social worker with the pointy high heels said I was wrecking the family and that if I kept things up the way they were going, with my bad behavior getting all of the attention, my parents were going to lose my sister too. I knew I was bad, I wasn't crazy though. (p. 6)

Confusing Gender Variant Youth with Gay or Lesbian Youth

Gender variant young people frequently have been confused with youth who are gay or lesbian. In fact, many of the same diagnostic criteria used to justify a diagnosis of GID are also supposed "cues" to a gay or lesbian identity. Some gay boys play with girls, enjoy girl toys, have effeminate mannerisms, and avoid rough-and-tumble play. Some young lesbians enjoy playing with the boys, play sports and games associated with boys, possess mannerisms and speech associated with boys, and dress in typical boy clothing. The biggest difference, and a critical one, is that gay boys and lesbian girls generally do not express dissatisfaction with their gender—that is, their sense of maleness or femaleness. In some cases, children with limited information about their emerging gay or lesbian identity may speak about *wishing* that they were a boy or a girl, but seldom do they state that they *are* a boy or a girl. The following case illustration represents an example of this misperception:

> Damond is a 10-year-old Latino child who was referred because his therapist felt inadequate in treating what he described as a transgender child. Damond lives with his mother, her second husband, a younger sister, and an older brother in a two-bedroom, middle income housing project in Brooklyn, New York. A therapist at a community mental health clinic sees both Damond and his mother. Damond is bright, very verbal, and precocious.
>
> The interview, which consisted of Damond, his therapist, his mother, and me [the interviewer], began with a series of questions initiated by Damond. Who was I? Was I a doctor? Why was I interested in seeing him? I answered directly and honestly and then proceeded with my own questions. First, given that he was a bright child, what were his career ambitions? He asked if he could draw his answer on his own pad of paper that he had with him. He drew a naked boy.
>
> When I asked what his drawing represented, he informed me that he wanted to be the first nude male dancer. He suggested that if he were a naked dancer, then boys would like him. He then went on to explain that first he would need "the operation" because the only way he could get boys to like him was if he was a girl.

He then asked if he could share a secret with me and, when I agreed, he wrote on another piece of paper, "I am gay." He also inquired as to whether I was gay, and then whether his therapist was gay. We all answered. He also was clear, when probed, that he did not see himself as a girl, but felt that to get boys to like him, he needed to become a girl and for that he would have to have "the operation."

Based on this interview, this child did not seem to be transgender, but a child who may be gay and in need of some accurate information about sexual identity development. The interview raised other concerns that I discussed with the therapist for further, unrelated treatment.

In this case, Damond most likely was not transgender, because he seemed comfortable in his gender identity and self-identified as gay in his sexual identity. Other cases may not always be so clear. It is just as important that transgender children and youth are not mislabeled as gay or lesbian, although they frequently self-label as such prior to coming to a full understanding of their transgendered nature. Similarly, LGB young people must not be mislabeled as transgender. Coming to understand the experiences of transgender persons is a complex phenomenon that requires specialized training and supervision from a trained and skilled trans-affirming social worker. Practitioners who listen carefully to the narratives of their young clients and who do not permit their own negative judgments about transgender persons to misguide them are the most effective, and appropriately neutral. The following section provides further recommendations for child welfare practice with transgender children, youth, and their parents.

What Can Youth Workers Do?

Youth workers who are unfamiliar with transgender young people's issues need guidance about how to proceed. The following recommendations provide a foundation for practitioners interested in enhancing their practice with transgender youth, and their parents.

Youth-serving professionals should begin by educating themselves about transgender youth. Practitioners should not wait until they have a transgender young person in their office to seek out information. Books, especially those written by transgender persons (several of which have been identified in this chapter), are extremely useful ways of gathering information about transgender persons. Films that portray transgender persons through a nonpathological lens, most specifically *Ma Vie en Rose* (Berliner & Scotta, 1997), the brutal but true story of Brandon Teena in *Boys Don't Cry* (Peirce & Bienen, 1999), and the 2005 release *Transamerica* (Tucker) can be extremely informative and enlightening. Professional articles in print journals can also be educational. The plethora of internet resources provides a rich array of information. As bibliotherapy has been proven to be useful with clients, many of these materials—print, video, and virtual—can also be shared with clients to increase their information and knowledge.

Youth-serving professionals must assist parents in resisting outright electroshock, reparative, or aversion-type treatments. There is never a justification for using these approaches to "treat" gender variance or GID. These are unethical and dangerous practices and inappropriate interventions to use. Residential programs that offer to turn trans children into "normal" children should be avoided, because they do more harm than good. Most of them have been disavowed by major professional organizations, including but not limited to the American Psychiatric Association, the American Psychology Association, the National Association of Social Workers, and the American Association of Marriage and Family Therapists.

Treatments for depression and associated conditions should not attempt to enforce gender stereotypical behavior but should focus on practice from a trans-affirming perspective. The goal should be to help the clients to get at, and eliminate, the depression or other condition. In these situations, it is always important to assess what part systemic reactions—i.e., those of parents, schools, churches, peer groups, etc.—play in contributing to the presenting depression. Often, when the systems change, the depression lessens.

Youth-serving professionals should assist parents in developing mutually acceptable compromise strategies, which can include negotiating with the gender variant youth to dress in modified gender clothing for formal events such as weddings, but permitting the youth to dress androgynously for school and peer activities. Young people who use opposite-gendered names should be permitted to use the name of their choice.

Parents and young people must work with practitioners to keep communication open. All young people, irrespective of gender issues, need love, acceptance, and compassion from their families. It is one of the things they fear losing the most. Youth need to be reminded that their parents' love for them is unconditional.

Youth workers need to be able to identify resources for trans children, youth, and families in the community, or be willing to take the risks necessary to create them (see Brill & Pepper, 2008).

Transgender children and youth should be assisted with developing strategies for dealing with societal stigmatization, name calling, and discrimination.

In completing an assessment of a transgender youth, professionals should be familiar with the criteria in DSM-IV for GID; be comfortable with discerning the differences between a gay, lesbian, bisexual, or questioning youth and a transgender youth; and use a modified version of Israel and Tarver's Gender Identity Profile (1997). The Transgender Health Program in Vancouver, British Columbia, has also provided a very comprehensive and well written set of guidelines for the *Clinical Management of Gender Dysphasia in Adolescents* (de Vries, Cohen-Kettenis, & Delemarre-Van de Wail, 2006). A companion publication from this same organization entitled *Ethical, Legal, and Psychosocial Issues in Care of Transgender Adolescents* (White Holman & Goldberg, 2006) should be very useful reading for all social workers.

Practitioners should be aware that transgender young people are part of every culture, race, religion, class, and experience.

Transgender young people of color and their families face compounded stressors resulting from transgender phobia, prejudice, and racism, and may need additional emotional and social support, as well as legal redress of discrimination.

Youth workers should make sure that all individual, self-help, family, and group treatment approaches are appropriate for intervening with a transgender child and his or her family (Swann & Herbert, 2009).

Practitioners must be aware of the possibility that violence both within and outside of the child's family might be directed toward the transgender child. Sexual violence, including rape, is also prevalent, and the practitioner should closely monitor the safety of the youth.

Youth workers must be ready to respond and reach out to siblings, grandparents, and other relatives of the transgender child to provide education, information, and support.

Practitioners should help parents understand that the gender variant child's behaviors and mannerisms are natural to them.

Practitioners should help parents to develop a strategy and sometimes a script for addressing the questions neighbors and members of the community may have about their transgender child. Schools, social service, child welfare systems, mental health systems, and religious institutions all are likely to encounter gender variant youth. These organizations and the individuals who work within them need to identify consultants to act as trans-affirming professional guides and provide in-service training to assist them with the process of becoming trans-affirming systems. These systems must set about transforming their organizational cultures to include sensitive and welcoming services for all children, youth, and families (Mallon, 1998b). Child welfare systems that are residential in nature may have unique issues, and will need specialized training to care for transgender children, youth, and their families.

Child welfare organizations, youth-serving organizations, and state level policymakers must develop clear, written policies about hormone use for trans youth in their care. In most states, if a person is over 18, he or she may consent to his or her own medical or mental health treatment. In the absence of clearly stated policies, however, trans youth may use a variety of approaches, many of which may threaten or irreversibly harm their health. Youth-serving policymakers, with consultation from professionals in the field, must develop these guidelines in-house (see DeCrescenzo & Mallon, 2000). Failure to do so will result in youth developing their own individual policies, which may result in later litigation for the organization.

Gay, lesbian, bisexual, and questioning youth service providers must also work to respond to the unique needs of transgender young (Lev, 2004; Mallon, 2009). Most LGB organizations solely meet the needs of lesbian, gay and bisexual teens and young adults; services for trans youth should also be explored.

Practitioners must accept the reality that not everyone can provide validation for a transgender child or teen. Some will simply not be able to understand the turmoil and pain transgender children and youth experience. In these instances, practitioners must be prepared to vigorously advocate on behalf of these youth.

11

Other Special Populations within the Community of LGBTQ Youth

In addition to transgender youth, the LGBTQ community has other special populations who may need special attention from youth workers. These include homeless/runaway LGBTQ youth, questioning youth, and LBGTQ youth of color.

Homeless LGBTQ Youth

The U.S. Department of Health and Human Services estimates that the number of homeless and runaway youth ranges from 575,000 to 1.6 million per year (Robertson & Toro, 1998). In his analysis, Ray (2006) suggests that between 20% and 40% of all homeless youth identify as LGBT, and my own research (Mallon, 1998b, 1999) suggests an even a higher incidence (50%) of homeless youth identifying as LGBT. Several studies from Seattle, Los Angeles, and New York have suggested that more than 50% of the runaway and homeless youth populations surveyed identified as LGBT (Kruks, 1991; Mallon, 1998b; Seattle Commission on Children and Youth, 1988). See also *Lesbian, Gay, Bisexual and Transgender Youth: An Epidemic of Homelessness* (Ray, 2006).

Family conflict is the primary cause of homelessness for all youth, LGBT or straight. Specifically, familial conflict over a youth's sexual orientation or gender identity is a significant factor that leads to homelessness or the need for out-of-home care. According to one study, 50% of gay teens experienced a negative reaction from their parents when they came out and 26% were kicked out of their homes (Remafedi, 1987). My study (Mallon, 1998b) found similar results with 33% of youth reporting that they had been kicked out of their homes due to disclosure of sexual orientation. Another study (Thompson, Safyer, & Pollio, 2001) found that more than one-third of youth who are homeless or in the care of social services experienced a violent physical assault when they came out, which can lead to youth leaving a shelter or foster home because they actually feel safer on the streets (Mallon, 1998b, 1999).

Whether LGBT youth are homeless on the streets or in temporary shelter, they face a multitude of challenges that threaten their chances of becoming healthy, independent adults (Van Leeuwen, Boyle, Salomonsen-Sautel, Nico Baker, Garcia, Hoffman, & Hopfer, 2006).

Health and Mental Health Issues

Living on the streets puts the health of LGBTQ youth at constant risk. Runaway and homeless LGBTQ youth typically do not have ready access to health care that recognizes and addresses sexual concerns. In addition to the life-threatening consequences of HIV infection, substance abuse, and street violence, street youth often suffer from upper respiratory infection, body and pubic lice, burns, numerous injuries, sexually transmitted diseases, dermatological problems, and mental health problems. The extremes of temperatures, irregular sleep in exposed places, poor diet, propensity toward smoking cigarettes, and the lack of opportunities for regular showers exacerbates the problem. Hunger is also a serious problem for street youth.

As mentioned in Chapter 8, some young lesbians engage in sexual relationships with males and get pregnant. Pregnant teens who live on the street find their problems magnified. Prenatal care and living with a child on the street is an onerous prospect.

LGBT homeless youth are especially vulnerable to depression, loneliness and psychosomatic illness, withdrawn behavior, social problems, and delinquency. The fact that LGBT youth live in a society that discriminates against and stigmatizes LGBT people makes them more vulnerable to mental health issues than heterosexual youth (Mallon, 1998b). This vulnerability is only magnified for LGBT youth who are homeless.

Homeless LGBTQ youth are also at risk for more severe mental health problems. Street youth suffer primarily from anxiety and depression. Many have also suffered from childhood sexual, physical, or emotional abuse or other trauma related to family violence, as evidenced in the following quote from Sara, a 17-year-old Caucasian lesbian in Los Angeles:

> My family was always a mess. My mom's boyfriends were always disgusting. Most times they beat on her; sometimes they beat on my brothers and me. One of them molested me for years, starting when I turned 11. I didn't tell my mother—I mean she couldn't even help herself, how was she gonna help me? My life from the time I was 5 until the time I left home at 15 was a nightmare. Believe it or not, running away from home was the best thing that ever happened to me. But I still have a lot of bad s**t that haunts me about all the stuff that happened to me.

As evidenced by the above exchange, at times the psychological stress is more than many young people can endure. Some LGBTQ youth reportedly make suicide attempts to escape from the isolation and estrangement they feel. One Toronto youth named Buzz recalled:

> I was high every day. My life was a mess, I hated myself. I had nothing. I didn't have a family that cared for me, I didn't have a home, I didn't have anyone I thought I could go to. I tried to kill myself three times. They always tried at the shelter to give me a referral for counseling, but I never went. I never trusted them. Finally after a pretty serious

suicide attempt—I sliced up my arm with a razor blade—I was hospitalized. When I was released from the hospital they found me a good place to stay and things have been better since then.

Substance Abuse

The combination of stressors inherent to the daily life of homeless youth leads some to abuse drugs and alcohol. Several studies found that between 10% and 20% of homeless youth self-identify as chemically dependent (Baer, Ginzler, & Peterson, 2003; McMorris, Tyler, Whitbeck, & Hoyt, 2002; Unger, Kipke, Simon, Montgomery, & Johnson, 1997). These risks are exacerbated for homeless youth identifying as lesbian, gay, or bisexual. Personal drug usage, family drug usage, and the likelihood of enrolling in a treatment program are all higher for LGB homeless youth than for their heterosexual peers (Cochran, Stewart, Ginzler, & Cauce, 2002; Olson, 2000).

Risky Sexual Behavior

All homeless youth are especially vulnerable to engaging in risky sexual behaviors because their basic needs for food and shelter are not being met. Defined as "exchanging sex for anything needed, including money, food, clothes, a place to stay or drugs" (Greene, Ennett, & Ringwalt, 1999, p. 1406) survival sex is the last resort for many LGBT homeless youth. Those who identify as LGBT, according to one study (Greene et al., 1999), were three times more likely to participate in survival sex than their heterosexual peers, and 50% of homeless youth in another study (Cochran et al., 2002) considered it likely or very likely that they will someday test positive for HIV.

Frank is an 18-year-old bisexual Latino "system kid" who has lived on the streets of New York City for many years. His story illustrates many of the reasons and risks for LGBT street youth:

When I was about 7 or 8 I went into foster care placement. My mother was like majorly into drugs, she was like burnt out and she neglected us a lot and a lot of the neighbors saw that and there was a lot of complaints made and so [the child welfare agency] ended up coming to the house and finding my mother not there, or going there and finding my mother there but finding no food in the house, or finding the house a mess, you know, or finding drug paraphernalia, or finding drug behavior of some type, you know, so we were placed in foster care. We were taken in and out of foster homes a lot—taken away, then given back to my mother four months in, then given back three months in, and then given back a week in, and then given back, you know, and then as we got older it progressed, it got worse. I mean we went from going to foster homes to going to group homes, to going to boarding schools, to going to [city youth] facilities, to going to lock up, to going to [a detention center], and then to going to jail upstate.

I was about 16 when I was released from jail and that's when I hit the streets. I couldn't go home—didn't have a home, I wasn't going to go back to a group home, I just kinda started to hang out, you know, staying at friend's houses, finally I started to just spend more and more time on the streets. I spent a few nights in shelters, but then I'd either get fed up with the rules or kicked out for getting into conflicts with other residents—to be honest it didn't always have to do with my sexuality.

I started to like a lot of the things I found out on the street, I mean I started hustling at that point—you know, prostitution—and in the beginning I thought that I wasn't going to be able to get into this, then I ended up liking it, you know, and getting into it. I made a lot of money. But I also got into drugs, big time—coke, heroin, hard stuff—I guess it's hereditary. I did it all out there. About two months ago I took the HIV test, and found out that I'm HIV positive. Sometimes folks in the drop-in center try to help me get it together and there's times when I'd like to get it together, you know, to have a home, but then I think—maybe it's too late for me.

Victimization of Homeless LGBT Youth

LGBT youth face the threat of victimization everywhere: at
home, at school, at their jobs, and for those who are out-of-
home, at shelters and on the streets. A study by Kipke, Simon,
Montgomery, Unger, and Iverson (1997) found that LGBT
homeless youth are seven times more likely than their heterosexual peers to be victims of a crime. While some public safety
agencies try to help this vulnerable population, others adopt a
"blame the victim" approach, further decreasing the odds of
victimized youth feeling safe reporting their experiences.

LGBT Homeless Youth in the Justice Systems

LGBT youth who are part of the juvenile and criminal justice
systems are frequently victims of harassment and violence due
to their gender/sexual orientation (National Center for Lesbian
Rights [NCLR], 2006). For example, respondents in one small
study (Curtin, 2002) reported that lesbians and bisexual girls
are overrepresented in the juvenile justice system and that they
are forced to live among a population of other youth who are vi-
olently anti-LGBT. Gay male youth in these systems are also
emotionally, physically, and sexually assaulted by staff and other youth (NCLR, 2006).

Transgender Homeless Youth

Transgender youth are disproportionately represented in the
homeless population. More generally, some reports indicate
that one in five transgender individuals need or are at risk of
needing homeless shelter assistance. However, most shelters
are segregated by birth sex, regardless of the individual's gender identity, and homeless transgender youth are even ostra-
cized by some agencies that serve their LGB peers.

What Can Youth Workers Do?

Although LGBTQ street youth have some unique service provi-
sion needs, most require the same services as their non-gay
counterparts. Among the services that street youth require are

direct services on the street; drop-in center services; and shelter and transitional living services.

Direct Services on the Street

Life on the streets is a transient and shifting scene. Before programs are initiated, workers must survey the street scene to determine the "turf," to figure out who hangs out where. Although there is blending, LGBTQ street kids hang out in different areas in different cities than do non-LGBTQ street youth. In urban areas street work begins by visiting youth-oriented gathering areas—parks, street corners, "strolls" (areas where LGBTQ youth are known to prostitute), and specific neighborhoods or restaurants that are tolerant of LGBTQ life and where LGBTQ youth are known to hang out. Youth may also hang out around bus or train terminals, or fast food restaurants, because they are open late at night. Peep shows, bars, and transient hotels are also places where LGBTQ street youth may congregate. In rural and suburban areas, youth hang out in different types of places. For example, in rural farming areas, homeless youth hang out in cornfields where it is easy to stay without being observed.

Street workers need to assess their safety levels on the street. Two-person teams are ideal. They create a partnership and workers feel less isolated. Although safety is paramount, hanging out regularly is the first step to becoming part of the street scene.

In some areas LGBTQ street youth may seem invisible and indistinguishable from other street youth. However, when this group is observed by workers who are knowledgeable about LGBTQ people, they can be differentiated from the others. Most importantly, street workers must learn to listen to youth. Young people who live on the streets have a very low level of trust for adults; many have been used by adults and trust will have to be earned.

Able-Peterson and Bucy (1993) offer several rules for engaging homeless youth.

Rule #1: First and foremost, street workers must learn young people's names. Young people feel important when someone has taken the time to connect and learn their names. Use whatever name they give you—street youth use nicknames regularly. Do not press them to disclose their real name with you in the earliest stages of a developing relationship. It is also important to repeat your name to them every time you see them, so that they will get used to hearing and using yours. People are not strangers if they are using first names. It is also important to remember that every new person is viewed with suspicion.

Rule #2: It is essential that street workers state very simply who they are, and with whom they are connected. In working with LGBTQ street youth, workers must be especially attuned to their unique culture and language. Many workers carry cards with their names and their agency's name and services printed on them. Cards distributed should refer to services that are specific to LGBTQ youth. Introductory assessment questions should be utilized in a conversational manner. Emphasize the ability you have to connect them with food, clothing, showers, and medical care. Repeat your name and theirs when you say good-bye.

Rule #3: Street workers need to be patient and consistent. Engagement and relationship building with street youth takes time. Young people who have survived on the streets know that it is their wariness that has kept them alive. Street workers need to be clear that what they offer (food, clothing, shelter) comes with no strings attached. Although trust is developed slowly, there is an easy camaraderie on the streets. After a worker has bumped into a youth three or four times, the young person begins to get used to the worker's presence and may begin to form a relationship with him or her.

Rule #4: Workers need to trust the process. There are no short cuts to relationship building. As the relationship develops between the youth and the street worker, so usually will the requests for assistance. Case management, resource identification, and advocacy often begins on the streets, but may move into the drop-in center as time, need, and the relationship progress.

Drop-In Centers

The drop-in center provides a transition from the work conducted on the streets and longer term services. Drop-in centers
are places where youth can take a shower, get clothes, meet
with a counselor, attend a life skills group, participate in a
GED class, take part in a recreational activity, have a meal,
and begin to deepen relationships. Drop-in centers are usually
located near areas where youth hang out. Some centers also
have medical vans attached to their programs and provide
much needed health care for youth on the streets. LGBTQ
youth who have spent a great deal of time on the streets might
be initially reluctant to participate in drop-in center activities
because of past negative experiences with insensitive social
services providers. Peer outreach is key to ensuring that the
center is a safe place for all youth.

Shelters and Transitional Living Programs

Since 1974, shelters have been an important part of the array of
services available to street youth. LGBTQ youth, many of whom
have experienced very poor fits in the child welfare system,
might avoid shelters or transitional living programs at all costs.
Although family reunification is a major goal in child welfare,
policymakers lack a true understanding of the needs of street
youth and the reasons why many LGBTQ young people do not
live at home. Reunification may be possible for many homeless
young people, but for others, it must be acknowledged that this
is not a realistic or practical goal. It is important to realize that
crisis intervention and residential care for young people whose
separation from their family will become permanent is very different from interventions with first-time runaways. In most cases, individual host homes, rather than a shelter, may be a
preferable alternative for less street-wise youth.

Shelters and host homes that are committed to providing
care for LGBTQ youth must consciously focus on creating an
affirming and supportive environment to ensure safety for all
young people. At the very minimum, shelter staff and host
home volunteers at all levels should be knowledgeable and

trained about LGBTQ culture and norms; agency literature should include references to welcoming and working with LGBTQ persons; and health and mental health care providers must be able to say through their language and their actions that they are comfortable and confident in working with LGBTQ youth. Shelters that do not create an affirming environment for LGBTQ youth will not be utilized by them.

Transitional living programs (TLPs), funded by the Family and Youth Services Bureau, are usually single apartments rented by multiservice youth-serving organizations in the community to house homeless youth. TLPs are excellent program models for adolescents who are moving toward self-sufficiency. In addition to providing stable, safe living accommodations while a homeless youth is a program participant, these programs also provide an array of services necessary to assist homeless youth in developing both the skills and personal characteristics needed to enable them to live independently. Among these services are education, life skills development, information, and counseling aimed at preventing, treating, and reducing substance abuse among homeless youth and appropriate referrals and access to medical and mental health treatment. Youth may live in this supervised living arrangement for up to 18 months.

Like adult homelessness, LGBTQ youth homelessness is not simply a matter of identifying housing for a young person. Nor should youth homelessness be viewed entirely as an indicator of problem youth behavior, but as evidence of society's inability to develop adequate supports for youth and families troubled by economic hardship, substance abuse, gender/sexual orientation issues, incest, and familial violence. All runaway and homeless youth face a multitude of problems when on the streets. LGBTQ youth are further burdened by lack of family support, unsafe child welfare placements, and societal heterocentrism and homophobia. The dual stigmatization of being LGBTQ and homeless can lead to an overwhelming sense of despair and hopelessness. Making mainstream runaway and homeless youth services accessible to LGBTQ youth is an active, ongoing, and evolving process that requires organizational sensitivity and responsiveness. Homeless LGBTQ youth can be moved from the streets into appropriate homes if they are provided with competent practitioners to work with them, and if programs are designed to sensitively meet their needs.

Questioning Youth

Questioning youth, in my clinical experience, fall into three main categories:

1. Youth who are "going through a phase" or experimenting, exploring their sexuality—a normative process for all young people—are considered questioning youth. Some youth are more comfortable exploring their sexuality and gender than others. In some cases, this exploration may be due to a specific living situation, such as a single-gendered group home, a juvenile justice facility, or even a single-gendered high school. The term *situational homosexuality* is explained in Chapter 1, and may also be appropriate for use with those youth who may be questioning their gender or sexual orientation in same-gendered environments.

2. Youth who have experienced but may have not disclosed sexual abuse perpetrated by adults, particularly by adults of their same sex, may question their gender or sexual orientation. Young people who have been sexually abused may require more time to work out their sexual identity. Experiencing sexual abuse can cause confusion about sexual orientation. A youth may wonder if sexual abuse caused him or her to be gay, or may question his or her sexual orientation because of the abuser's gender. It is the role of the youth worker to reassure the young person that sexual abuse does not cause homosexuality. The worker will also need to keep in mind that the youth will need treatment for the sexual abuse first before they are able to fully explore issues of gender or sexual orientation. As the youth receives the appropriate treatment, their orientation will unfold. If youth workers are addressing issues of sexual abuse for the first time, they will need to report this information

based on the required protocol for their agency and the state's laws on mandated reporters.

3. Some questioning youth may have a serious psychiatric condition, and claim an LGBT identity to fit in. Youth who claim an LGBT identity may believe that doing so will provide them with group membership. Belonging is very important to all young people; to have an identity and group membership is what many youth long for. When youth claim an LGBT identity with these motivations, they usually later move on from this identity.

What Can Youth Workers Do?

In their curriculum, Elze and McHaelen (2009) again offer some helpful advice to youth workers to assist young people who are questioning their gender or sexual identities. In summary, they suggest:

- Youth workers should validate the youths' confusion. Let them know it is normal to be confused. Explore their confusion with them. What is the questioning about? Where does the questioning come from? Youth workers should be affirming and supportive.
- Youth workers should assess their level of information and provide accurate information, correcting myths and stereotypes as they come up. Youth workers may ask the youth what they know about being LGBT, what they've heard about LGBT people, where they've received this information, and what their concerns are.

In the best of circumstances, understanding and accepting one's sexual orientation and gender identity is an ongoing process that spans a number of years. Youth workers should always be respectful of a questioning identity and be clear that they are not in the business of pushing youth toward premature resolution of sexual and/or gender identity. Instead, be available to answer youths' questions, help them process information, and direct them to additional information should they request it.

LGBTQ Youth of Color

The successful development of healthy group and self identities among members of oppressed groups involves the ability to reconcile competing demands from the dominant society and the individual's minority community—whether ethnic, racial, or LGBT. Research has demonstrated that positive LGBT self and group identities, as well as a positive racial or ethnic identity, are integrally connected to psychological well-being (Walters & Old Person, 2008). Despite the recognition that ethnic or LGBT identity is important in mental health functioning, little research has investigated the multiple oppressed statuses and the interactions of those statuses on psychosocial functioning among LGBT youth of color. For these youth the integration of a consolidated racial and LGBT identity are even more complex, involving negotiations of conflicting allegiances to the LGBT communities and ethnic communities. Despite the importance of understanding the complex interactions among racism, sexism, and heterosexism that LGBT youth of color must negotiate, the youth work practice literature remains inadequate in providing any practice guidelines that incorporate these issues.

As members of more than one minority group, LGBTQ youth of color face special challenges in a society that often presents heterosexuality as the only acceptable orientation. Economic and cultural disparities, as well as sexual risk taking and other sometimes dangerous behavior, make these youth vulnerable to HIV, pregnancy, and sexual violence. Holistic, culturally competent health care is essential to their well-being.

Black and Latino youth in one study (Grov & Bimbi, 2006) did not differ from white youth in acceptance of their own sexuality, but while LGBTQ youth of color develop similarly to white youth, they must bear the twin burdens of racism and homophobia.

To simply cluster all lesbian, gay, bisexual, and transgender youth of color into a homogenous category is misleading. LGBT youth of color come from very diverse backgrounds—American

Indian, African American, Latino/a, Asian American, and others—and, as a result, there is greater diversity within groups than there is between groups. Additionally, it must be recognized that there are a myriad of self- and community-designated terms for sexual and gender identity and expressions (e.g., *queer* or *two spirit*). There is also a fluidity in gender and sexual identities and constructs. As a result, *LGBT* as a term is used as a placeholder, an umbrella term to cover culturally specific terms and understandings of sexual and gender identities; e.g., *two-spirit* in American Indian communities, *ambiente* among Latinos, or *same-gender loving* among African Americans. Accordingly, it is imperative that youth workers who use this section as a guide to practice with diverse communities be sure to properly assess terminology and associated cultural and spiritual meanings for the individual and groups they are working with and utilize culturally specific understandings to frame interventions and community building.

Youth of color are significantly less likely to have told their parents they are LGBTQ: one study found that while about 80% of LGBTQ whites were out to parents, only 71% of Latinos, 61% of African Americans, and 51% of Asians and Pacific Islanders were out to parents (Grov & Bimbi, 2006).

LGBTQ youth of color also report feeling pressure to choose between their ethnic and their sexual identities; these youth are less likely to be involved in gay social and cultural activities than their white counterparts (Battle, Cohen, Warren, Fergerson, & Audam, 2000).

What Can Youth Workers Do?

Youth workers engaging LGBTQ youth of color need to be aware of the multiple issues faced by these young people. Youth workers must be aware that LGBTQ youth of color may have different issues regarding coming out to families, and negotiating identities in communities where they live and interact. For a fuller understanding of these multiple issues, workers should refer to the report by Bridges (2007) which documents the impact of homophobia and racism on LGBTQ youth of color.

12

Conclusions: A Call for Organizational Transformation

Over the past few years, several authors have enumerated the needs of LGBTQ youth and identified the obstacles that youth-serving agencies face in addressing their needs. This final chapter, using the experiences of several nationally known LGBTQ-affirming agencies, offers recommendations on agency philosophies concerning the reality of LGBTQ youth and additionally offers suggestions on ways to create safe, welcoming, and nurturing environments.

The dilemmas faced by LGBTQ youth and their families are clear. Youth-serving agencies, already challenged by many substantial issues, tend to exhibit a range of sensitivities to LGBTQ youth. At one extreme, some agencies openly discriminate against LGBTQ youth; at the other end of the spectrum, agencies are affirming in their approaches and strongly advocate for their needs. Most youth-serving agencies fall somewhere in the middle. Many agencies initiate good faith efforts to become more affirming, but this usually occurs when they come across their first openly LGBT youth. A more proactive stance, and preparation working with diverse groups of youth, rarely happens without a precipitating incident.

Youth-serving agencies come into contact with LGBTQ youth for several reasons: family conflict, health or mental health of the youth, school problems, or out-of-home placements. The scope of these issues, as reviewed in this book, requires that all youth-serving agencies become knowledgeable about and sensitive to the needs of LGBTQ youth. The vulnerability of LGBTQ youth, particularly at times when they come to the attention of youth-serving agencies, is yet another reason that youth providers should be prepared for working with this population. The most inopportune time to increase one's knowledge about a service population is when they arrive at the agency in a crisis and are in need of immediate assistance.

Efforts to increase sensitivity to LGBTQ youth cannot be sustained in an environment that does not explicitly encourage such undertakings. As agencies struggle to demonstrate their commitment to diversity, they must also be willing to include sexual orientation in that diversity continuum. In doing so, they begin the work necessary for creating a safe and welcoming environment for all clients, not just LGBTQ youth. Once this orientation is set, and the organization's culture shifts to clearly include LGBTQ concerns, it becomes possible for youth workers to learn about, advocate for, and provide affirming services to LGBTQ youth.

While it is a reality that some agency administrators and boards might object to specific LGBTQ sensitivity awareness or programs particularly geared toward the population, fewer should take exception to overall approaches designed to increase worker competence in working with clients who are underserved.

Transforming the Organization's Culture

Transformation is a powerful word, but nothing less is needed to create programs that are responsive to the needs of LGBTQ youth. Appreciation of diversity is a key element in this process. The examination of an organization's commitment to diversity is a common theme for all youth-serving agency administrators. Diversity approaches in organizations have utilized various strategies to increase worker competence in meeting the needs of a variegated client population, including in-service training, nondiscrimination policies, culturally specific celebrations, advocacy, client/staff groups that explore diversity, and efforts to encourage a climate that welcomes all people. An LGBTQ approach could be integrated into any one of these areas. A community-based youth center commemorating Latino History Month with a potluck dinner representing dishes from various Latino countries could just as easily celebrate Pride Month by inviting a speaker to discuss the events that led to the civil rights struggle for the LGBTQ community.

Youth-oriented agencies must also be committed to creating a safe environment for all youth. The enactment of a zero tolerance policy for violence, weapons, emotional maltreatment, slurs of all types, and direct or indirect mistreatment conveys to all clients that their safety is a priority. A strong stance against violence of all types, including verbal harassment, sends an important message to all youth. It says, "We will try to protect you, and you will not be blamed for being yourself. Those who offend are the ones who will be dealt with, because their behavior is unjustified and unacceptable."

All youth benefit from youth workers who are open, honest, and genuine. Everyone benefits from philosophies that indicate an agency's willingness to address difficult issues head on. Giving clients and staff permission to raise controversial topics signals that all people associated with the agency will be treated with respect and dignity.

It is only through intentional and deliberate organizational cultural shifts—true transformation—that a climate supportive of LGBTQ youth can be developed. Several agencies across the United States and in Canada have been successful in creating organizations where LGBTQ youth are welcomed, feel safe, and have their needs met. This does not take huge amounts of money, tremendous time commitments on the part of staff, or other extraordinary efforts. It does, however, take commitment from board members, administrators, and other key organizational players—including the youth and their families.

What Can Youth-Serving Agencies Do?

Supportive Employees

An organization that is responsive to the needs of LGBTQ youth must be staffed and administered by people who demonstrate a similar commitment to providing services that foster self-esteem and acceptance for LGBTQ youth. To achieve this, the organization must aim to hire open-minded, supportive employees, including openly LGBT professionals. Organizations must communicate antidiscrimination policies in hiring, and must be honest about recruiting and maintaining LGBT employees. Hiring openly LGBT employees sends a clear message that the agency is demonstrating its commitment to LGBTQ youth. Although hiring LGBT staff is critical, it should not be assumed that every LGBT adult is knowledgeable about working with LGBTQ youth, or appropriate for working with them. All staff, regardless of sexual orientation, should be assessed for their appropriateness in working with youth, and then educated about LGBTQ youth, the problems that they experience in society, and how to effectively support them. Hiring non-LGBT staff that are comfortable with LGBTQ clients and open to being educated about working with this population is also an essential part of this process.

With increasing openness about gender/sexual orientation, clients often ask employees about their sexual orientation. Some child welfare agencies have encouraged staff to be open about their orientation, because ambiguity about staff's orientation led to mistrust in the youth. Once staff were clear, youth stopped playing guessing games and started to do the work that they had come to the agency for in the first place.

One of the most positive outcomes of recruiting openly LGBT staff reported by several of the agencies was that staff turnover was at an all-time low rate. Being able to be employed in an accepting atmosphere is a great employee benefit for LGBT adults.

In-Service Training

In-service training, integrated into the overall training efforts of the organization, is critical in providing quality services to LGBTQ youth and families. As with all issues of diversity, integrating real-life case examples into the training sessions can make the educational process come alive for workers. Helping staff to identify appropriate language, addressing the common myths and stereotypes that most people have about LGBTQ people, replacing the myths with accurate information about the population, and creating environments that suggest safety— these are all good first steps. However, training efforts should be tailored to meet the individual needs of staff members from various disciplines (see Elze & McHaelen, 2009).

Helping staff to identify resources in the community and to assess their own personal heterocentrism are also critical factors in the training process. Use of videos and guest speakers—especially LGBTQ youth or their parents—can be particularly effective in getting the message across.

Transferring abstract information learned in training sessions into actual intervention techniques takes practice. Participation in a variety of exercises assists staff members in beginning to develop a set of appropriate and unconstrained responses. Staff members are intentionally exposed to situations that lead to self-reflection. For example, in one training focusing on the maladaptive coping responses that can be associated with hiding one's sexual orientation, the participants were asked at the start of the session to write their most personal secret on a slip of paper, to fold it, and to place it under the chair that they would be sitting on all day. Without ever being asked to share what they wrote, the message is powerful. In ensuing discussion, attitudinal change and understanding of the consequences of secrecy often begins to evolve.

Providing staff at the training with written information, resources, and other materials ensures that the educational process continues after the training session is finished. This process should be monitored and evaluated by program supervisory staff.

Welcoming Strategies

The creation of a physical environment that welcomes LGBTQ youth, families, and prospective employees is as significant as staff training. Again, these efforts do not need to cost a great deal of money, but evidence of them signals acceptance and safety.

The organization's waiting room is probably the most important place to start this process. Reading materials, symbols, and signs that specifically spell out the organization's attitude about respect for all people will be noticed and will help clients, their families, and employment applicants feel welcome.

Many agencies hang posters in their waiting rooms that signal acceptance. One agency in New York specifically developed nine colorful, gender-neutral posters that announce an LGBTQ-affirming environment. The messages that these send are intentionally subtle. LGBTQ organizations will also be able to provide organizations with pamphlets; others can be downloaded from the internet.

The presence or lack of books focusing on LGBTQ issues also conveys important messages. Thousands of LGBTQ-related books might also be purchased in bookstores both brick-and-mortar and online.

Integrated Policies and Public Information Materials

Although LGBTQ people have experienced greater acceptance and understanding in the past 30 years, many organizations may still actively discriminate against LGBTQ youth. In other cases the organization's inattentiveness to the needs of LGBTQ youth will send a clear signal that they are not welcome. Reviewing an organization's policies and public materials can assist the organization in consistently attempting to provide sensitive services to all youth.

An organization's commitment to LGBTQ youth involves more than posters and books. It is critical to recognize that the internal structure of the organization, as reflected in its policies and public information materials, may also need to be evaluated.

Training and educational efforts may assist staff in developing their competence in working with a particular population, but policies and what the outside community knows about the organization may also need to be altered in order to effect real change.

Advocacy Efforts

Recognizing that the environment outside the organization is often actively hostile to LGBTQ youth, youth-serving agencies must be committed to external change and advocacy efforts as well. This may mean, for example, participating in an advocacy campaign to end discriminatory language in contracts or attending human services-related conferences. Affirming organizations must also be prepared to advocate for LGBTQ youth in community schools, in local adolescent treatment settings, and in families. Further, organizational leaders must also be prepared to educate local and state politicians and funders about the needs of LGBTQ youth.

As the 21st Century progresses, youth workers continue to play a critical role in developing young people. Youth work has historically had a cyclical interest in certain subjects: youth suicide, violence, substance abuse, and homelessness. All are worthwhile issues that require our best efforts, but the needs of LGBTQ youth should not be viewed as the "issue du jour" of youth work. Sexual orientation issues are too vital to continue to be overlooked. A particular LGBTQ client might trigger a plethora of attention at the time, only to fade from view when the next issue presents itself. Dealing with LGBTQ youth issues in an intermittent manner is a mistake. Organizations must continue to diligently develop training, assess their own ability or inability to respond to the needs of LGBTQ youth, and address new approaches to competent practice with these youth and their families. For an organization to be consistently sensitive to the needs of its clients, efforts to create affirming environments and to transform existing ones must be realized. If organizations are guided by the same principles that embrace diversity, and can translate these into concrete action, LGBTQ youth will be better served.

References

Able-Peterson, T., & Bucy, J. (1993). *The street outreach training manual*. Washington, DC: U.S. Department of Health and Human Services.

Alyson, S. (1991). *Young, gay, and proud*. Boston: Alyson Press.

American Psychological Association. (1994). *Diagnostic and statistical manual of mental disorders* (4th ed.). Washington, DC: Author.

Baer, J., Ginzler, J., & Peterson, P. (2003). DSM-IV alcohol and substance abuse and dependence in homeless youth. *Journal of Studies on Alcohol, 64*(1): 5–14.

Battle, J., Cohen, C.J., Warren, D., Fergerson, G., & Audam, S. (2002). *Say it loud I'm black and I'm proud: Black pride survey 2000*. New York: National Gay and Lesbian Task Force. Available from www.thetaskforce.org/reports_and_research/black_pride.

Bartlett, N. H., Vasey, P. L., & Bukowski, W. M. (2000). Is gender identity disorder in children a mental disorder? *Sex Roles, 43*(11/12), 753–785.

Berliner, A. (Director, Cowriter), & Scotta, C. (Producer). (1997). *Ma vie en rose* [Film]. Available from SONY Classics, Los Angeles.

Bernstein, R. (2003). *Straight parents, gay children: Keeping families together*. Cambridge, MA: Da Capo Press.

Bridges, E. (2007). *The impact of homophobia and racism on GLBTQ youth of color*. Washington, DC: Advocates for Youth. Available from www.lgbt.ucla.edu/documents/ImpactofHomophobiaandRacism_000.pdf.

Brill, S., & Pepper, R. (2008). *The transgender child: A handbook for families and professionals*. New York: Cleis Press.

Bullard, L., Owens, L.W., Richmond, L., & Alwon, F. (Eds.). (2010). Residential issues in child welfare [Special issue]. *Child Welfare, 89*(2).

Burgess, C. (2009). Internal and external stress factors associated with the identity development of transgender youth. In G. P. Mallon (Ed.). *Social services for transgendered youth* (2nd ed.) (pp. 35–48). New York: Routledge.

Carrera, M. (1984). *Sex: The Facts, The Acts, and Your Feelings*. New York: Random House.

Carrera, M. (1992). *The Language of Sex: An A to Z Guide*. New York: Facts on File.

Cass, V. C. (1979). Homosexual identity formation: A theoretical model. *Journal of Homosexuality, 4*, 219–235.

Cass, V. C. (1984). Homosexual identity formation: Testing a theoretical model. *The Journal of Sex Research, 20*, 143–167.

Chauncey, G. (1995). *Gay New York: Gender, urban culture, and the making of the gay male world, 1890–1940*. New York: Basic Books.

Cochran, B., Stewart, A., Ginzler, J., & Cauce, A. (2002). Challenges faced by homeless sexual minorities: comparison of gay, lesbian, bisexual, and transgender homeless adolescents and their heterosexual counterparts. *American Journal of Public Health, 96*(5), 773–777.

Colapinto, J. (2000). *As nature made him: The boy who was raised as a girl*. New York: HarperCollins.

Coleman, E. (1981.) Developmental stages of the coming out process. *Journal of Homosexuality, 7*(2/3), 31–43.

Cooper, K. (2009). Practice with families of transgendered youth. In G. P. Mallon (Ed.). *Social services for transgendered youth* (2nd ed.) (pp. 111–31). New York: Routledge.

Criswell, E., & Bedogne, M. (2002). *Out in the cold* [film]. Denver, CO: Matthew Shepard Foundation.

Currah, P., Juang, R.M., & Minter, S.P. (Eds.). (2006). *Transgender rights*. Minneapolis, MN: University of Minnesota Press.

Curtin, M. (2002). Lesbian and bisexual girls in the juvenile justice system. *Child and Adolescent Social Work Journal, 19*(4), 285–301.

Davis, C. (2008). Social work with transgender and gender non-conforming persons. In G.P. Mallon (Ed.) *Social work practice with lesbian, gay, bisexual, and transgender people* (pp. 212–242). New York: Routledge.

DeCrescenzo, T. (Ed.). (1994). *Helping gay and lesbian youth: New policies, new programs, new practices*. New York: Haworth Press.

DeCrescenzo, T., & Mallon, G. P. (2000). *Serving transgender youth: The role of child welfare systems*. Washington, DC: CWLA Press.

De Monteflores, C., & Schultz, S. J. (1978). Coming out: Similarities and differences for lesbians and gay men. *Journal of Social Issues, 34*(3), 59–72.

DeSetta, A. (2003). *In the system and in the life: A guide for teens and staff to the gay experience in foster care*. New York: Youth Communication.

De Vries, A. L. C., Cohen-Kettenis, P. T., & Delemarre-Van de Waal, H. (2006). Clinical management of gender dysphoria in adolescents. *In Caring for Transgender Adolescents in BC: Suggested Guidelines*.

Vancouver, British Columbia, Canada: Transgender Health Program. Available from http://transhealth.vch.ca/resources/library/tcpdocs/ guidelines-adolescent.pdf.

Dreifus, C. (2005, May 31). Declaring with clarity, when gender is ambiguous. *New York Times*, p. D2.

Elze, D., & McHaelen, R. (2009). *Moving the margins: Curriculum for child welfare services with LGBTQ youth in out-of-home care.* Washington, DC: National Association of Social Workers & Lambda Legal. Available from www.lambdalegal.org/publications/moving-the-margins/moving-the-margins.html.

Eudey, B. (n.d.). *Resource materials for the handbook for achieving gender equality through education.* Available from http://gend4100 unittwo.wetpaint.com.

Fairchild, B., & Hayward. N. (1998). *Now that you know: A parents' guide to understanding their gay and lesbian children* (Updated Ed.). New York: Mariner Publishers.

Feinberg, L. (1993). *Stone butch blues.* Ithaca, NY: Firebrand Books.

Foucault, M. (1976). *The history of sexuality, Vol. 1.* Victoria: Penguin Books.

Garnets, L., Hancock, K. A., Cochran, S.D., Goodchilds, J., & Peplau, A. (1991). Issues in psychotherapy with lesbians and gay men: A survey of psychologists. *American Psychologist, 46,* 964–972. Available from www.apa.org/pi/lgbt/resources/issues.aspx.

Glenn, W. (2009). "For colored girls": Reflections of an emerging male to female transgender and gender variant youth consciousness. In G.P. Mallon (Ed.) *Social work practice with transgender and gender variant youth* (2nd ed.) (pp. 83–94). New York: Routledge.

Greene, J.M., Ennett, S.T., & Ringwalt, C.L. (1999). Prevalence and correlates of survival sex among runaway and homeless youth. *American Journal of Public Health, 89*(9), 1406–1409.

Griffin, E.W., Wirth, J.W., & Wirth, A.G. (1997). *Beyond acceptance: Parents of lesbians and gays talk about their experiences*. (Rev. ed.). New York: St. Martin's Griffin.

Grov, C., & Bimbi, D.S. (2006). Race, ethnicity, gender, and generational factors associated with the coming out process among gay, lesbian, and bisexual individuals. *Journal of Sex Research, 43*(2), 115–121.

Guzman, M.R., & Bosch, K.R. (July 2007). High-risk behaviors among youth. *Neb Guide*. Lincoln, NE: University of Nebraska-Lincoln Extension, Institute of Agriculture and Natural Resources. Available from www.ianrpubs.unl.edu/epublic/live/g1715/build/g1715.pdf.

Hamer, D., Hu, S., Magnuson, V.L., Hu, N., & Pattatucci, A.M. (1993). A linkage between DNA markers on the X chromosome and male sexual orientation. *Science, 261*(5119), 321–327.

Hooker, E. (1957). The adjustment of the male overt homosexual. *Journal of Projective Techniques, 21*, 18–31.

Hooker, E. (1967). The homosexual community. In J. Gagnon & W. Simon (Eds.), *Sexual deviance* (pp. 380–392). New York: Harper & Row.

Israel, G., & Tarver, D. (1998). *Transgender care: Recommended guidelines, practical information and personal accounts*. Philadelphia: Temple University Press.

Kinsey, A.C., Pomeroy, W.B., & Martin, C.E. (1948). *Sexual behavior in the human male*. Philadelphia: W.B. Saunders.

Kinsey, A.C., Pomeroy, W.B., Martin, C.E., & Gebhardt, P. H. (1953). *Sexual behavior in the human female*. Philadelphia: W.B. Saunders.

Kipke, M., Simon, T., Montgomery, S., Unger, J., & Iverson, E. (1997). *Journal of Adolescent Health, 20*, 360–367.

Kruks, G. (1991). Gay and lesbian homeless/street youth: Special issues and concerns. *The Journal of Adolescent Health, 12*(7), 515–518.

Lambda Legal Defense and Education Fund. (2001). *Youth in the margins: A report on the unmet needs of lesbian, gay, bisexual, and transgender adolescents in foster care.* New York: Author.

Langer, S.J., & Martin, J.I. (2004). How dresses can make you mentally ill: Examining gender identity disorder in children. *Child and Adolescent Social Work Journal, 21*(1), 5–23.

Lev, A.I. (2004). *Transgender emergence: Therapeutic guidelines for working with gender-variant people and their families.* New York: Haworth Press.

LeVay, S. (1993). *The sexual brain.* Cambridge: MIT Press.

LeVay, S., Baldwin, J., & Baldwin, J. (2009). *Discovering human sexuality.* Sunderland, MA: Sinauer Associates.

Mallon, G.P. (1994). Counseling strategies with gay and lesbian youth. (pp. 75–91). In T. DeCrescenzo (Ed.), *Helping gay and lesbian youth: New policies, new programs, new practices.* New York: Haworth Press.

Mallon, G.P. (1998a). Lesbian, gay, and bisexual orientation in childhood and adolescence. In G. Appleby & J. Anastas, *Not just a passing phase: Social work with gay, lesbian, and bisexual people* (pp. 123–144). New York: Columbia University Press.

Mallon, G.P. (1998b). *We don't exactly get the welcome wagon: The experience of gay and lesbian adolescents in child welfare systems.* New York: Columbia University Press.

Mallon, G.P. (1999). *Let's get this straight: A gay and lesbian affirming approach to child welfare.* New York: Columbia University Press.

Mallon, G.P. (2001). *Lesbian and gay youth: A youth worker's perspective.* Washington, DC: CWLA.

Mallon, G.P. (Ed.). (2008). *Social work practice with lesbian, gay, bisexual, and transgender people* (2nd ed.). New York: Routledge.

Mallon, G.P. (Ed.). (2009). *Social work practice with transgender and gender variant youth* (2nd ed.). New York: Routledge.

Mallon, G., & Betts, B. (2005). *Recruiting, assessing and retaining lesbian and gay foster and adoptive families: A good practise guide for social workers*. London: British Association of Adoption and Foster Care.

Mallon, G.P., & DeCrescenzo, T. (2008). Social work practice with transgender and gender variant children and youth. In G.P. Mallon (Ed.) *Social work practice with transgender and gender variant youth*. (2nd ed.) (pp. 65–86). New York: Routledge.

Malyon, A.K. (1982). Psychotherapeutic implications of internalized homophobia in gay men. *Journal of Homosexuality, 7*(2/3), 59–69.

Martin, A.D., & Hetrick, E.S. (1988). The stigmatization of the gay and lesbian adolescent. *Journal of Homosexuality*, 15, 163–183.

McDougall, B. (Ed.). (2007). *My child is gay: How parents react when they hear the news*. (2nd ed.) New South Wales, Australia: Allen & Unwin.

McFadden, D., & Pasanen, E.G. (1998). Comparison of the auditory systems of heterosexuals and homosexuals: Click-evoked otoacoustic emissions. *Proceedings of the National Academy of Sciences, 95*(5), 2709–2713.

McMorris, B., Tyler, K., Whitbeck, L., & Hoyt, D. (2002). Familial and "on-the-street" risk factors associated with alcohol use among homeless and runaway adolescents. *Journal of Studies on Alcohol, 63*(1), 34–43. Available from http://digitalcommons.unl.edu/cgi/view content.cgi?article=1040&context=sociologyfacpub.

Mental Health America. (n.d.). *Factsheet: Bullying and gay youth*. Available from www.nmha.org/go/information/get-info/children-s-mental-health/bullying-and-gay-youth.

National Center for Lesbian Rights. (2006). *The legal rights of lesbian, gay, bisexual, and transgender youth in the juvenile justice system.* San Francisco: Author.

Olson, E. (2000). Gay teens and substance use disorders: Assessment and treatment. *Journal of Gay and Lesbian Psychotherapy, 3*, 69–80.

Pazos, S. (2009). Social work practice with female-to-male transgender and gender variant youth. In G.P. Mallon (Ed.) *Social work practice with transgender and gender variant youth.* (2nd ed.) (pp. 87–103). New York: Routledge.

Parents and Friends of Lesbians and Gays, Inc. (1990). *Why is my child gay?* Washington, DC: Author.

Peirce, K. (Cowriter & Director), & Bienen, A. (Writer). (1999). *Boys don't cry* [film]. Distributed by Fox Searchlight Pictures, Los Angeles.

Pharr, S. (1988). *Homophobia: A weapon of sexism.* Little Rock, AR: Chardon Press.

Ray, N. (2006). *Lesbian, gay, bisexual and transgender youth: An epidemic of homelessness.* New York: National Gay and Lesbian Task Force Policy Institute and the National Coalition for the Homeless.

Remafedi, G. (1987). Male homosexuality: The adolescent's perspective. *Pediatrics, 79*(3).

Remafedi, G., Farrow, J.A., & Deisher, R.W. (1991). Risk factors of attempted suicide in gay and bisexual youth. *Pediatrics, 87*(6), 869–875.

Remafedi, G., French, S., Story, M., Resnick, M.D., & Blum, R. (1998). The relationship between suicide risk and sexual orientation: Results of a population-based study. *American Journal of Public Health, 88*(1), 57–60. Available from http://ajph.aphapublications.org/cgi/reprint/88/1/57.pdf.

Robertson, M.J., & Toro, P.A. (1998). *Homeless youth: Research, intervention, and policy.* United States Department of Health and Human

Services. Available from http://aspe.hhs.gov/progsys/homeless/symposium/3-Youth.htm.

Rule, N.O., & Ambady, N. (2008). Brief exposures: Male sexual orientation is accurately perceived at 50 ms. *Journal of Experimental Social Psychology, 44*, 1100–1105.

Rule, N.O., Ambady, N., & Hallett, K.C. (2009). Female sexual orientation is perceived accurately, rapidly, and automatically from the face and its features. *Journal of Experimental Social Psychology, 45*, 1245–1251.

Ryan, C., & Futterman, D. (1998). *Lesbian and gay youth: Care and counseling*. New York: Columbia University Press.

Ryan, C., Huebner, D., Diaz, R.M., & Sanchez, J. (2009). Family rejection as a predictor of negative health outcomes in white and Latino lesbian, gay and bisexual young adults. *Pediatrics, 123*, 346–352.

Savin-Williams, R. (2001). *Mom, Dad, I'm gay: How families negotiate coming out*. Washington, DC: American Psychological Association.

Savin-Williams, R. (2006). *The new gay teenager*. Cambridge, MA: Harvard University Press.

Scholinski, D., with Adams, J.M. (1997). *The last time I wore a dress*. New York: Riverhead Books.

Seattle Commission on Children and Youth. (1988). *Report on gay and lesbian youth in Seattle*. Seattle, WA: Seattle Commission on Children and Youth.

Swann, S., & Herbert, S.E. (2009). Ethical issues in the mental health treatment of adolescents. In G.P. Mallon (Ed.), *Social services for transgendered youth* (2nd ed.) (pp.19–35). New York: Routledge.

The World Professional Association for Transgender Health. (2001). *Standards of care for gender identity disorders* (6th version). Minneapolis, MN: Author. Available from www.wpath.org/publications _standards.cfm.

Thompson, S.J., Safyer, A.W., & Pollio, D.E. (2001). Differences and predictors of family reunification among subgroups of runaway youths using shelter services. *Social Work Research, 25*(3).

Troiden, R.R. (1979). Becoming homosexual: A model of gay identity acquisition. *Psychiatry, 42*, 362–373.

Troiden, R.R. (1993). The formation of homosexual identities. In L.D. Garnets & D.G. Kimmel (Eds.), *Psychological perspectives on lesbian and gay male experiences* (pp. 191–217). New York: Columbia University Press.

Tucker, D. (Director). (2005). *Transamerica* [film]. Available from Weinstein Company, Los Angeles.

Unger, J., Kipke, M., Simon, T., Montgomery, S., & Johnson, C. (1997). Homeless youths and young adults in Los Angeles: Prevalence of mental health problems and the relationship between mental health and substance abuse disorders. *American Journal of Community Psychology, 25*(3), 371–394.

Van Leeuwen, J., Boyle, S., Salomonsen-Sautel, S., Nico Baker, D., Garcia, J., Hoffman, A., & Hopfer, C. (2006). Lesbian, gay, and bisexual homeless youth: An eight-city public health perspective. *Child Welfare, 85*(2), 151–170.

Walters. K., & Old Person, R. (2008). Lesbians, gay, bisexuals, and transgender people of color: Reconciling divided selves and communities. In G.P. Mallon (Ed.) *Social work practice with lesbian, gay, bisexual, and transgender people.* (2nd ed.) (pp. 41–68). New York: Routledge.

Weinberg, G. (1972). *Society and the healthy homosexual.* Garden City, New York: Anchor Press.

White Holman, N., & Goldberg, J. (2006). Ethical, legal, and psychosocial issues for transgender adolescents. *International Journal of Transgenderism, 9*(3/4), 95–110.

Wilber, S., Ryan, C., & Markamer, J. (2006). *CWLA best practice guidelines: Serving LGBT youth in out of home care*. Washington, DC: CWLA Press.

Wornoff, R., & Mallon, G.P. (Eds.). (2006). LGBTQ youth in child welfare [Special issue]. *Child Welfare, 85*(2).

Wren, B. (2000). Early physical intervention for young people with atypical gender identity development. *Clinical Child Psychology and Psychiatry 5*(2), 220–231.

LGBTQ Resources

Ambiente Joven
www.ambientejoven.org
Ambiente Joven is a project of Advocates for Youth and is dedicated to the gay, lesbian, and transgender Latino/a youth community in the United States and Latin America, with the goal of providing information about sexual and mental health, as well as general cultural information.

Children of Lesbians & Gays Everywhere (COLAGE)
www.colage.org
COLAGE is the only national and international organization in the world specifically supporting young people with LGBT parents.

Equity Project
www.equityproject.org
The Equity Project is an initiative to ensure that LGBT youth in juvenile delinquency courts are treated with dignity, respect, and fairness. The Equity Project examines issues that impact LGBT youth during the entire delinquency process, ranging from arrest through postdisposition.

Family Acceptance Project (FAP)
http://familyproject.sfsu.edu
FAP is a community research, intervention, education, and policy initiative that studies how family acceptance and rejection affects the health, mental health, and well-being of their LGBT children. FAP develops educational materials and resources for families and providers to help families support their LGBT children, and publishes research on LGBT young people and families. FAP is developing the first evidence-based family interventions to help ethnically diverse families decrease rejection and increase support for their LGBT children.

Family Equality Council
www.familyequality.org
The Family Equality Council works to ensure equality for LGBT families by building community, changing hearts and minds, and advancing social justice for all families.

Gay, Lesbian, Bisexual, and Transgender Youth Support Project
www.hcsm.org/glys/glys.htm
Provides training and technical assistance for providers and educators in Massachusetts who support LGBT youth.

Gay, Lesbian, and Straight Education Network (GLSEN)
www.glsen.org
GLSEN is the leading national education organization focused on ensuring safe schools for all students. Established nationally in 1995, GLSEN envisions a world in which every child learns to respect and accept all people, regardless of sexual orientation or gender identity/expression.

Lambda Legal
www.lambdalegal.org
Lambda Legal is a national organization committed to achieving full recognition of the civil rights of lesbians, gay men, bisexuals,

transgender people, and those with HIV through impact litigation, education, and public policy work.

Lambda Legal's Youth in Out-of-Home Care Project raises
awareness and advances reform on behalf of LGBTQ youth in
the child welfare, juvenile justice, and homeless systems of
care. The Project aims to increase the will and capacity of
youth-serving organizations to prepare and support LGBTQ
youth as they transition from adolescence to independence.
The Project works with LGBTQ youth as well as social workers,
case managers, administrators, and other child welfare advocates to ensure safe and affirming child welfare services for
LGBTQ youth.

National Center for Lesbian Rights (NCLR)
www.nclrights.org
NCLR is a national nonprofit, public interest law firm committed to advancing the civil and human rights of LGBT people
and their families. NCLR litigates precedent-setting cases at
the trial and appellate court levels; advocates for equitable
public policies affecting the LGBT community; provides free
legal assistance to LGBT people and their legal advocates; and
conducts community education on LGBT legal issues.

Since its inception in 1993, NCLR's Youth Project has
been educating service providers, advocating for policy
changes, providing legal information, and helping youth share
their stories; ensuring a brighter future for all LGBT young
people—in schools, at home, in foster care, and in the juvenile justice system.

Gender Spectrum
www.genderspectrum.org
Gender Spectrum provides education, resources, and training to
help create a more gender sensitive and supportive environment
for all people, including gender variant and transgender youth.

In a simple, straightforward manner, Gender Spectrum helps
students, families, schools, and organizations understand and

address the concepts of gender identity. Their accessible, practical approach is based on research and experience, enabling their clients to gain a deeper understanding of gender variance.

Hetrick-Martin Institute (HMI)
www.hmi.org
Since 1979, HMI, home of the Harvey Milk High School, has believed that all young people, regardless of sexual orientation or identity, deserve a safe and supportive environment in which to achieve their full potential. HMI creates this environment for LGBTQ youth between the ages of 12 and 21 and their families. Through a comprehensive package of direct services and referrals, HMI seeks to foster healthy youth development. HMI's staff promotes excellence in the delivery of youth services and uses its expertise to create innovative programs.

National Resource Center for Permanency and Family Connections
www.nrcpfc.org
The National Resource Center for Permanency and Family Connections at the Hunter College School of Social Work is a training, technical assistance, and information services organization dedicated to help strengthen the capacity of state, local, tribal, and other publicly administered or supported child welfare agencies to institutionalize a safety-focused, family-centered, and community-based approach to meet the needs of all children, youth, and families, including LGBTQ children, youth, and families. The National Resource Center for Permanency and Family Connections is a service of the Children's Bureau, Administration for Children and Families, Department of Health and Human Services, and is a member of the One T/TA Network. For information specific to LGBT child welfare issues, visit www.hunter.cuny.edu/socwork/nrcfcpp/info_services/lgbtq-issues-and-child-welfare.html.

National Youth Advocacy Coalition (NYAC)
www.nyacyouth.org
NYAC is a capacity building organization that advocates for
and with LGBTQ young people in an effort to end discrimination against these youth and to ensure their physical and
emotional well-being. NYAC builds the capacity of organizations that serve LGBTQ youth through technical assistance,
resource sharing, and youth engagement.

Opening Doors Project
www.abanet.org/child/lgbtq.shtml
The Opening Doors Project, a project of the American Bar
Association's Center on Children and the Law, aims to increase
the legal community's awareness of LGBTQ youth in foster
care and the unique issues they face, and provide the legal
community with advocacy tools to successfully represent these
youth. The American Bar Association Center on Children and
the Law is a full-service technical assistance, training, and research program addressing a broad spectrum of law and court-
related topics affecting children and youth.

One-in-Teen Youth Services Nashville
www.one-in-teen.org
Since 1989, One-in-Teen Youth Services has provided a safe
space for LGBTQ youth, between the ages of 14 and 21, to be
themselves. Basic services are free, and events are alcohol and
drug free.

Parents, Families & Friends of Lesbians and Gays (PFLAG)
www.pflag.org
PFLAG promotes the health and well-being of LGBT people
and their families and friends through support, to cope with
an adverse society; education, to enlighten an ill-informed
public; and advocacy, to end discrimination and to secure
equal civil rights.

Safe Schools Coalition
www.safeschoolscoalition.org
The Safe Schools Coalition is a public-private partnership in support of LGBT youth to help schools—at home and all over the world—become safe places where every family can belong, where every educator can teach, and where every child can learn, regardless of gender identity or sexual orientation.

Sexual Minority Youth Assistance League (SMYAL)
www.smyal.org
SMYAL assists LGBTQ youth in Washington, DC. It promotes self-confident, healthy, productive lives for LGBTQ youth as they journey from adolescence into adulthood. It concentrates in five areas: life skills and leadership development, counseling and support, health and wellness education, safe social activities, and community outreach and education.

The Trevor Project
www.thetrevorproject.org
Based in California, the Trevor Project operates the only nationwide, around-the-clock crisis and suicide prevention helpline for LGBTQ youth.

The World Professional Association for Transgender Health (WPATH)
www.wpath.org
WPATH is a professional organization devoted to the understanding and treatment of gender identity disorders with 500 members from around the world, in fields such as medicine, psychology, law, social work, and counseling.

YouthResource
www.youthresource.com
YouthResource, a website created by and for LGBTQ young people ages 13 to 24, takes a holistic approach to sexual health by offering support, community, resources, and peer-to-peer education about issues of concern to LGBTQ young people.

About the Author

Gerald P. Mallon DSW is a professor and executive director of the National Resource Center for Permanency and Family Connections at the Hunter College School of Social Work in New York City. Dr. Mallon also works closely with the State of Louisiana, where he has done extensive work in the Louisiana child welfare system in the aftermath of Hurricanes Katrina, Rita, and Gustav.

For more than 35 years, Dr. Mallon has been a child welfare practitioner, advocate, educator, and researcher. His most recent publications include: *Social Work Practice with Gender Variant and Transgender Youth; Social Work Practice with Lesbian, Gay, Bisexual, and Transgender People; and Lesbian and Gay Foster and Adoptive Parents: Recruiting, Assessing, and Supporting an Untapped Resource for Children and Youth.* In 2010, Dr. Mallon was honored as the Child Advocate of the Year by the North American Council on Adoptable Children.

Dr. Mallon earned his doctorate in social welfare from the City University of New York at Hunter College and holds a master's degree in social work from Fordham University and a bachelor's degree in social work from Dominican College.

Dr. Mallon has lectured and worked extensively throughout the United States, and internationally in Ireland, Cuba, Indonesia, Australia, Canada, and the United Kingdom.

Correspondence may be sent via e-mail to gmallon@ hunter.cuny.edu.

175